Also by Bonnie Borromeo Tomlinson:

STOP BUYING BINS
& other blunt but practical advice
from a home organizer

Praise for
STOP BUYING BINS
& other blunt but practical advice
from a home organizer

"I liked the tone of this author. I could almost picture her standing right next to me stating these very direct ideas and well-earned pearls of wisdom. Plus the writer is very funny."

"This is one of the greatest books about paring down and organizing that I've ever read. The personal stories are touching and inspiring. The author is very humorous too."

"Everyone should read this book! It has great lessons on how to keep your life in order which translates not only to things but to mental health as well."

"This book is a game changer! It's engaging and funny while also offering sustainable solutions. It is helping me find motivation to simplify!"

"Your book is so well written, and reads like a conversation you would have with an obviously bright friend. I have so many decluttering books, and I'm always hoping I will hit on just the right one that will fix me once and for all. This is it."

"This is a great read! Super enjoyable and an ultimately effective book. The processes are ruthless in the best ways, but not lacking compassion. And I laughed and laughed."

"I would hire her services in a heartbeat and this book is the next best thing."

"I just finished this book and will be reading it again, immediately! I found myself laughing, reflecting, getting inspired, and picking my jaw up off the floor! I'm so excited to be implementing her techniques! A must read for anyone with any amount of possessions!"

"Great easy read book that helps you develop a different mindset. I've read a lot of organizing books. This is one of my favorites."

"I have read SO many books on decluttering, organizing, etc. This is the most fun and motivating book of them all! Everyone has issues and Bonnie gives clear and easy ways to help with yours. If you want long-term solutions that will make your life better forever, read this book!"

"I read this book and loved it. I'm quite picky, and I thought everything about it was great, the topics, the fun tone, the prose, the design, the layout. The biggest compliment I can give is that I closed the book, and filled a big sack with clothes and brought it to the Salvation Army. That is just the beginning of my motivation post-reading."

"Amazing book about organizing, spoken with both wit and tough love. As a professional organizer myself, many of the stories I can relate to. This book is an easy read and a must for anyone wanting to better manage their clutter!"

"I'm a newbie professional organizer and I've been reading as much as I can about the business. OMG, what a great book! I've read a lot of books and yours, hands down, was my favorite and I never wanted it to end. I appreciate your wit and tough love approach. Can we be best friends?"

"This is truly an excellent book. I've read several books on organizing, minimizing, decluttering, but this one was really the best one yet. It is because the author talked about the psychological aspects of organizing and decluttering which is very important. We have such attachments to certain things for certain reasons and that is what the author is talking about. It was also entertaining at the same time."

"I just spent the morning reading through your book. Excellent, psychologically wise advice about reframing clients' mindsets about their stuff. I love your common sense advice."

"This is a laugh-out-loud read, but also had me in tears in many places. This author translates her experience as a home organizer into relatable stories and ultra helpful bulleted lists to frame an emotionally fraught topic into digestible and actionable bites. Highly, highly recommend this book."

"By far the best ever book for decluttering and staying that way! Loved the way the book is written in stages of decluttering. You actually feel like you are there and she is talking to you! I will read this book again just in case I missed anything and simply for pleasure!"

"If you have a clutter problem, you will find yourself in the chapters of this book. I LOVED this book! The author makes so many good points and insights that result in a reappraisal of why we keep what we keep. Thank you so much for writing this book."

"This is one of the best books I have read. I appreciate the author's bluntness but there is also a lot of compassion for her clients and readers. Her advice is sound, thorough, and easy to follow. There is a lot of good information in this book. Strongly recommend it."

"This is the book I have needed for years. Twenty some years of storing stuff has now been put on notice now that I have the tools to get rid of so much that is taking up room. This book has given me ways to face boxes of things that have overstayed their welcome and I am ready to start."

"Bonnie Tomlinson offers a no-nonsense, humor laden approach to managing your home and belongings. She has exceptional chapters on 'how to' edit and manage the project, some of the best ideas I have seen, and she breaks down processes very well. She has wonderful ideas on donating items that will appeal to most readers who feel guilty filling garbage dumps with their overabundance of stuff."

"Twenty-two years into being a mom, and three children later, I have accumulated quite the collection of 'things'. I found *Stop Buying Bins* on Amazon on the same day I had just run out to purchase (yet another) storage bin. The irony wasn't lost on me. *Stop Buying Bins* is concise and easy to read. Once I was able to understand the why, I was able to free myself from what was making me hold onto years of clutter. Bonnie has truly mastered the process and lays it all out in a simple, step-by-step guide for her readers. Her book is honest and real, a refreshing and inspiring read that reads as if she's talking to me."

"You may find yourself in some of these pages. I did and it made me reflect on my life. The writing was great, like I was having a talk with a friend."

"She has a great writer's voice. I would certainly like to meet her in person. She's got a great sense of humor!!!"

"Bonnie, the title of your book made me laugh out loud because it's so true! I know a few people who can use this book so I'll be picking up multiple copies."

"Bonnie sets just the right tone, and through her stories she makes you think deeply about your own clutter and desired changes. I've read a lot of books about clutter and decluttering, but Bonnie is the organizer I would hire if I could. I think it would actually be fun to work with her and I believe she would be a friend by the time we were done."

"Love Bonnie's salty style. She's spot on with her observations on the why of overconsumption and the why of breaking the cycle."

"You know a decluttering and organizing book is good when you set it down in the middle of chapter to overhaul your closet!"

"This was the most helpful book I've read about downsizing (and I've read many). It was well-written. Several times I laughed out loud: 'Bins give you the impression that you are organized when all you've actually done is box your garbage.' I look forward to more books by this author!"

"I've read at least a half dozen books about home organization. *Stop Buying Bins* is my favorite. I was inspired to begin purging within minutes of reading this. Thank you, Bonnie, if you publish another book, perhaps on decorating, I'll buy that one, too."

"Finally, a concise read, non judgemental, and the wonderful sense of humor we with too much stuff need. No shaming, just a reality check. Excuse me, I have a junk drawer I need to attend to!"

"If you do not know where to start, this book is step one."

STOP PUSHING PERFECTION

& just create a home
you can actually keep neat

Bonnie Borromeo Tomlinson

Yellow Lab Press
AMHERST, MASS

Copyright Disclaimer:
The information and advice contained in this book are based upon the personal and professional experiences of the author. The publisher and author are not responsible for any consequences resulting from the use of any of the suggestions, preparations, or procedures discussed in this book. Names and identifying details have been changed and fictionalized to protect the privacy of any individuals. In all cases, the retelling of these personal events are composites of multiple projects worked on by the author.

Copyright © 2023 by Bonnie Borromeo Tomlinson

All rights reserved. No part of this book may be reproduced or transmitted in any form or by any means, electronic or mechanical, including photocopying, recording, or by any information or retrieval systems, without the permission of the publisher.

Printed in the United States of America.

Editor: Jodi Simons
Book and cover design: David W. Edelstein
Author photograph: Yellow Lab Press

Yellow Lab Press
Amherst, MA 01002

Library of Congress Control Number: 2021921933

ISBN: 978-1-7378818-2-7 (paperback)
ISBN: 978-1-7378818-3-4 (ebook)

Subjects:
Nonfiction | How-To | House and Home |
Self-Help | Organizing | Cleaning
HOM019000

For Gilly

In Loving Memory of
Athena,
the yellow lab of Yellow Lab Press.
November 15, 2013 - April 28, 2022

Acknowledgments

Gratitude is an undervalued emotion, one that over time I've attempted to make a part of my daily life—from a wave in my rearview mirror to the guy who let me merge in front of him, to acknowledging that someone's mere presence in the universe has changed my life in miraculous butterfly-effect ways. I have much to be grateful for and I continue to attempt to never miss a moment to tell those people I value most just how much I appreciate them.

Thank you doesn't seem a big enough sentiment to express how grateful I am to all my friends and family and new supporters who purchased *STOP BUYING BINS*, read it, reviewed it, posted about it, told other people to buy it, and just lifted me up with compliments and praise. I've been blown away since day one of this writing journey. And having said that, there are some friends who are owed special recognition.

To Denise Mangiaracina Strafaci, my friend of 40+ years, who is always a source of support in my darker moments. Your strength, warmth, and resilience are all qualities you possess in spades. To have had you in my corner is a true blessing. To have had it for four decades is a miracle. Thank you, my friend.

To Felicity "Flick" Moore, whom I don't even remember meeting because we were old friends from the start. I believe your personal promotion of my last book is the single reason it started to sell internationally. And your humor, generosity, and effortless chic make me aspire to be more like you. Truth! Thank you, my dear.

To Serenity Kelly, and other inspiring friends like her who have offered similar sentiments: "I keep saying it but I'm just so proud of you and really in awe of you. You just did it! You packed up, you moved yourself to a totally new place, you followed your dream and you made it happen! That takes grit, determination, strength, and a set of boobs (because they are not weak like balls)! You, my friend, are amazing!" I don't even know what to say! If I am any of those things it is because I have surrounded myself with incredible individuals who bring it out in me because they themselves exemplify those qualities.

To my daughter, Gillian Tomlinson. An incredibly bright and creative person who will someday change the world with her work. My everyday life is in the building of a legacy you can be proud of. I love you more than words can express.

And thank you all. I am who I am because of you.

Why You Should Read This Book: A Note from the Author

I published a book last year called *STOP BUYING BINS*. Some of you may have read it. Of course, as the author of said book, I request you pick it up and read it as it sets the stage for this one. In it I explain techniques for downsizing household excess told through stories of individual client projects. It's not required reading to understand what you are about to read, but downsizing *is* the first step to organizing. It's worth a look. I'm really very proud of it.

For this book, I wanted to move from downsizing your clutter to organizing what's left. Along the way I hope to impart some quick tricks, tools of the trade, and essential lifestyle systems to make your day-to-day run smoother and keep your house in order. The goal here is not to live within the professionally staged pages of a home decor and design magazine, as lovely as that might seem, but rather:

- **to consistently have a neat and efficient household where precious time and money are not being wasted searching for or buying again those things you already own,**

- **to accomplish household tasks in less time with less labor,**
- **and to have room and energy to move within your four walls.**

* * *

Two years ago I moved from a large family house in Maryland near Washington, DC, to a stand-alone townhouse in Western Massachusetts. It's half the size and has two closets in the entire house!

More than likely you don't have this issue. Even my first apartment, a studio in Hoboken, NJ, had ample storage—a huge clothes closet, a stand-in pantry, plus a good-sized linen closet in the surprisingly spacious bathroom. *Side story: when I moved in, the previous renters had left a gigantic wicker peacock chair and matching side table, and there was still room for an ottoman—all in the bathroom.* But I digress. Here in my new home, without the luxury of storage space, I've learned some valuable lessons about **how to make the most of having less**, which also has the surprising byproduct of gratitude. I mentioned gratitude in my acknowledgments for good reason. When you love the space you live in, you rarely want for more and you appreciate what you have. This frees time for life's true priorities—relationships, mental and physical well-being, hobbies and interests, even just breathing in peace.

Now take a deep breath and let's get started.

Contents

Introduction... 1

1. If You Can't Find Me, I'm Hiding in the Bathroom 5

2. And If You Look Left, You'll See the Formal Living Room & Dining Room............................. 37

3. Please Remove Your Shoes........................ 65

4. Don't Go in There, My Room's a Mess............. 87

5. The Game Is On!.................................. 135

6. Mommy, Can I Have Friends Over for a Playdate? 161

7. I Don't Cook; The Kitchen's for Show.............. 181

8. Can You Ever Really Have Too Many Books? 215

9. Look at That! I Can See the Floor!................. 237

10. Where Did I Put That Thing? 261

Extras 283

How to Streamline Housework 283

*It Bears Repeating: Excerpt from Chapter 1 of
"Stop Buying Bins"*..................................... 288

My Take on Swedish Death Cleaning.................... 291

Keep Your Disorganized Life to Yourself 299

An Organized Life Simplifies........................... 302

Introduction

Living an organized life is not difficult. Too many people think that keeping things neat and tidy requires a lot of time, work, and stressful commitment. Admittedly at first it might seem that way as new systems are put in place and new habits are formed. But like anything else, practice makes perfect.

The first few times you attempt any new skill, you are bound to be thinking more about the steps involved than the task itself. Learning to tie your shoes, cook a meal, drive a car are all tasks that at first seem like a lengthy how-to list, but over time become skills so second nature to you that they involve little to no thought at all. In fact, with proficiency comes the ability to not only do one multistep procedure from muscle memory, but also a second task at the same time: tie your shoes while telling a story, cook a 3-course meal all at the same time, drive a car while maybe we should stay away from multitasking while driving. Suffice to say, learning new ways to live efficiently in your home will one day result in having an orderly space by sheer habit, and all while listening to your favorite podcast.

But I want to be honest with you. It's unlikely that your interior space will be so fine-tuned that it will look like #luxeathome on Instagram, certainly not if people live in your house. Those photos are fake. People don't live in those photos. Those rooms are rearranged and perfectly lit so the owner lounging on a chaise is ensconced in effortless chic. Little do you know that just out of the frame is a cacophony of designer pillows and tchotchkes to readjust the color combos to suit the photographer's vision. Then once the camera crew leaves for the day, that room will no longer look photo worthy. In fact, by the time you see it in a magazine, it will have been touched up even more so it is even further removed from reality. I say this to let it be known here and now, that the goal of this book is not to achieve that. I can show you how to create that look if you really want to know, but then you're going to have to rope that room off and hope dust never settles on anything. That's not organizing. That's staging. And it lasts less than 24 hours.

Unfortunately, staging is what far too many home organizers do. They would have you believe you CAN live in an enviable after-photo. You just have to purchase all new color-coordinated bins, label every surface in glitter marker, and always have the exact number of bottled waters in the refrigerator no matter how many you drink. And with all due respect to one notable celebrity in this field, unless all your clothes are a size 0 and you only wear variations on beige, your closet will never look like theirs, no matter how much joy is in it. **Remove from your mind the idea that perfection is your purpose.** Yes, it is true that once you are organized, things will be neater and tidier, but your intention here is to gain more time and space and comfort, not have your fruit lined in size formation. With that said, let me give you three quotes for the project ahead:

"Perfection is not the intention."
"Create a home that's neat, not neurotic."
"An organized life simplifies."

FACT: You CANNOT get your house organized without breaking some bad habits.
And you CANNOT keep it organized without creating some new ones.

So let's take these room by room. For each space we will discuss **practicality, efficiency, routine building,** and lastly, consider **decor**. It is my hope that by the end of this book, you will not only have learned some practical ways to put your possessions in order and learned how to keep them that way but also, more importantly, you have found a new life balance through an organized and simplified life. Label maker optional.

1

If You Can't Find Me, I'm Hiding in the Bathroom

I am an extroverted introvert. "What does that mean?" you ask. It means that I am not shy. I can hold my own in most conversations. And I can talk a blue streak if I've got a good rant going. But being social depletes my energy, and I need a break from people to recharge. As the laptop sticker my daughter bought me reads, "It's Too Peopley Outside." I think that's as close to a personal catchphrase as I could get.

When I'm at a party or some other social event, if I am nowhere to be found you can more than likely find me in the bathroom. A perfect little private space, alone, with no one to bother me other than the other introverts trying to find a place to escape to, too. As a result, I've seen the inside of a lot of bathrooms. Some fully energized me with their crisp and clean qualities while others just depleted me further. Those in the latter category were likely dirty, dimly lit, or crowded with dust-covered bric-a-brac. Add to the scenario having to wipe my hands on a decorative finger towel not intended for actual use, and this bathroom time has worn down my battery even further.

A bathroom, first and foremost, serves a practical purpose. By design it is a space to tend to one's personal hygiene, which means it needs to be kept as clean as possible. Sanitary. Sterile. Stocked with supplies. *No one ever wants to be caught with that last square of toilet paper and no backup roll within reaching distance.* And as beautiful as it may be to adorn your bathroom with objet d'art, unless you plan on cleaning these pieces regularly, expect them to become gunk-covered quickly. Between the humidity from the shower, hair, dust, and aerosol products, these items will be furry and/or sticky in no time. Yes, that quintessential basket of seashells that has taken its place of honor on many a toilet tank is a thing to seriously consider purging if you expect to keep your bathroom pristine. But let's forget about decorating for the moment and just talk toothpaste, shall we.

PRACTICALITY. We all have a general understanding of what one NEEDS in a bathroom. But let's play a little game by listing what we DON'T.

- Products you bought, used once, and either did not like or never worked into your routine.

- Towels made of fabric that is not absorbent.
- Mini trash cans that, while cute, provide insufficient space for what accumulates in a day.
- Anything with crusty dried goop under the cap.
- Anything collecting dust.
- Anything expired.

If you are in the habit of purchasing bath and beauty products that you try and never use again, then get in the habit of passing them along to friends, your neighborhood Buy Nothing Facebook page, your local donation center, etc. Storing unused products is not getting you closer to the serene bathroom of your spa dreams.

EFFICIENCY. Let's take practicality one step further and talk about making the space efficient. And the best way to do that is to streamline.

- How many towels do you own? How many do you really use?
- Do they match? Do you have complete towel sets—bath/hand/washcloth? Do you actually use complete towel sets?
- Do you have decorative towels that are NOT for use at all?
- And how are you hanging them—towel bars, hooks?
- Where and how are they stored?

- What about your personal hygiene products, medication, makeup, beauty supplies—are you using them, rotating them, checking for expiration regularly, storing them properly?
- Are they located for easy, user-friendly access?
- And all the same questions with regard to the cleaning supplies you use for the space.

Is your head spinning yet? I did say earlier that it takes a bit of work upfront to make it easier ever after. And all these things do make sense in the big picture. If you've got a family of five using one bathroom, and you only have one towel bar, it's a safe bet you need some alternative hanging options. *Doorknobs don't count.*

ROUTINE. How do you plan on maintaining this newly organized space? There are more things to consider.

- How often will you give your bathroom a quick clean? A deep clean?
- How often will you launder towels?
- How often will you refill your supplies?
- How often will you rotate out anything past its prime such as meds with expiration dates, seasonal supplies like sunscreen, moldy rubber ducks?

SIDE STORY: Dispose of said ducks after your child has gone to sleep and then immediately take that trash out. It's surprisingly distressing for a four-year-old to find a plastic friend, no matter how gross, in the garbage can under a mountain of trash. *Don't ask how I know that.*

DECOR. Okay, we have circled back. You don't live in a hospital so you are going to want some decor in your bathroom, but you are going to want to consider the following:

- Fabrics: Window treatments dense enough for privacy, if needed. Floor coverings for absorption, skid resistance, and comfort for bare feet. Both preferably machine washable. Stay away from multiple layers of fabric (toilet seat covers, tissue box cozies, layers of ornate dry clean only draperies). And please, for goodness sake, no decorative towels with satin ribbons and roses. If you can't use them to wipe your hands, what's the point?

- Knick Knacks: If they can't be rinsed off or Windexed clean, stay away from them. Safe to stay with natural materials like stone or pottery, or unbreakable plastics. Stay away from glass; shattered glass and bare bodies don't make a good team. Remember the shells I mentioned before? I'm going to give you a little leeway here and say go ahead but proceed with caution. Stop yourself short of a collection en masse in a basket. Both because of dust and difficulty in cleaning. Opt instead for one or two large shells just sitting on their own.

- Plants: They love the moisture from the shower and they clean the air at the same time. They will get dusty too so wipe down the leaves every once in a while.

- Artwork: I myself love huge framed artwork in a bathroom. I also dust weekly. I'll leave the final decision with you.

My advice? Keep it simple and washable. I'm not here to tell you what to do exactly but one suggestion I'd like to offer is that you should feel free to think outside the bathroom=water=blue-coastal-theme box. That goes for those of you actually living at the water's edge too. As cute as dolphins or as steadfast as lighthouses may be, mix it up. My childhood bathroom had cartoon dog wallpaper that I wish to this day I could find because I'd use it now. *Although I would never have had the decorative dog-shaped soaps that my mother had on a glass shelved display. Talk about dust! I mean, how do you wash off soap?*

* * *

If you've ever thought that the way you live is no big deal, that your interior space, its form and function, or even the color on the walls is not important, then you would be sadly mistaken. It affects everything—your physical, emotional, and psychological mood and well-being. Your surroundings are vital to your health so do yourself a favor—**consider how a space makes you feel and adjust accordingly.**

That's exactly what I did for June. I had the privilege of working with her and her husband some years back. He was using a walker and then a wheelchair in his final years and she had called me in to make adjustments to the furniture layout in their condo so he could better manage the space and, as she described it, "stop clipping the furniture." After he passed, she called me back to help transition her home into something more to her tastes.

June lived in a beautiful two-bedroom/two-bathroom condo in an assisted living community in Frederick, MD. Her building in particular was designed with wide halls and doorways for residents who needed wheelchair access. With her husband's passing she no longer needed the space but it was lovely to have just the same. She had been on her own for about six months and was finally feeling ready for this change.

"I want to redo the whole place, but over time and on a budget. I really want to start with my bathroom, which I hate with a passion. Paul made the decorating decisions and I wanted to make him happy, but God love him, the man had no taste. The wall color, the towels, all of it was what he wanted so I just went with it. How could I say no? Now that he's gone, every time I use the bathroom, it makes me sick and I'm starting to resent him for it. I know how terrible that sounds."

What June was referring to was the yellowish brown bathroom off her bedroom still littered with medical equipment. As mentioned earlier, the room was large enough to maneuver a wheelchair around and into the shower. It was void of any rugs or mats for that reason. A legged bed tray filled with Paul's prescription medicine bottles sat on the vanity between the double sinks. The towels were shades of white and gold with brown flowers and in various stages of being rendered useless due to bleach holes. And the toilet had a brown fuzzy toilet lid cover to match the toilet mat that wrapped around the base.

"I know. It's bad," she said with a grimace as she led me inside.

I smiled and said, "All I see is a blank slate and a jumping off point. So what do you want to do? I'm excited to hear your ideas."

June proceeded to tell me her ideas for her turquoise, grey, and white modern spa oasis—a daydream of high-gloss stone and cascading waterfalls all wrapped in a fluffy white terry bathrobe. I wrote my notes, took my photos, discussed her budget, and told her the primary bathroom was a great place to start on her redecorating journey. I said I'd get back to her with my plans in a few days.

"In the meantime, June, I would like to give you some homework," and **I broke down the following plan:**

- **Contact the pharmacist and ask how you should dispose of your husband's meds.**

- **Ask the condo association for guidance on how to donate or sell the medical equipment you no longer need, either to other residents or through an organization they work with.**

- **Collect all the towels, wash them, and donate. Or if you prefer, cut them up for rags.**

- **Go through all your products. Throw out any items that are expired or partially used that you have no use for. Give away any items you have not and will not use; that goes for personal hygiene and beauty products, small appliances like hair dryers, and cleaning supplies.**

- **Lastly, separate your everyday items from your occasional.**

"I'm on it," she said, already diving into the cabinets under the sink.

"Great! Then I'll let myself out and I'll call you in a few days."

* * *

Rarely does an organizer have the luck of working with someone more eager for change than themselves. But here I was with a client already jumping in, on all fours under her sink, while I was leisurely flipping through wallpaper samples at a local design studio. Even on her tight budget, I knew I could give her exactly what she asked for.

A few days later, as promised, I called her to say I was ready to present her with the details. She was having her hair done in DC and asked if I would mind meeting her at the salon. I was more than happy to oblige since I was already going to be downtown that day meeting with another client (see chapter eight). Once there, I showed her my ideas for everything from lighting to rugs and the wallcoverings in between. But, more importantly, I explained my reasons for each. As I've stated before, decorating in a space like a bathroom requires as its primary objectives attention to function and practicality. Rugs with non-skid backing, wallpaper and paint options resistant to mildew, accessories that are easy to clean. From the options I presented to her, she made her choices and the big picture was taking shape. With that part complete, the next step was to schedule the work. To keep her costs down, she said her son-in-law would do the painting and wallpaper. I had my reservations but she assured me his work was nearly professional.

Last item on our agenda was to discuss **my signature suggestion**. I like to leave a mark on each of my projects and I was hoping June would approve of this out-of-the-box suggestion. In her kitchen she had a wooden rolling center island. At just 2'x4' and three feet high, it was really too small to be efficient in her kitchen, but painted and put in the center of the bathroom rug in the center of the room, it would be a beautiful addition to hold her towels, candles, and a bouquet of fresh flowers to complete the spa theme. I suggested it be painted bright white.

"Really? Huh. But then what will I use in the kitchen?"

"Oh, you mean to hold that one red onion and scattered pages ripped out of Bon Appétit?" I said with a wink. "I'll find you something else when we get to the kitchen. Trust me on this. It's going to be gorgeous in the bathroom. Worst case scenario, we put it back."

"That's true. Okay. Let's give it a try!"

And that was a wrap. I left her to finish her hair and manicure, and ordered the wallpaper when I got back to the car. I texted her son-in-law the paint color for the walls and island and he replied that he'd take care of it in the evenings over the next week, which worked out perfectly with the delivery date of the wallpaper. He also agreed to install a few of the items I planned to use as part of the organizing plan, *as well as a bonus item I'll explain later in the chapter,* and that saved June even more money since I didn't have to call in my handyman. Everything was coming together.

* * *

Wouldn't it be so easy if all home redecorating/reorganizing projects started with an essentially blank slate where all one had to do was pull everything out, repaint, make modifications, clean, and put back only those items that were in line with your clear vision? Oh wait! That IS all redecorating/reorganizing projects!

"Wait what?!"

Yup! It's really that easy. **It just takes a clear goal and a bit of planning.** Here, I'll show you.

1. **Pull it all out.** Leave nothing behind—except of course what's attached.

2. **Look at your empty space and visualize two things—recall what made life more difficult in the space and ponder what would make your life easier.** Consider what it was about your previous arrangement that didn't work for you. Did you have to walk dripping wet

across the tile floor to the nearest towel bar after taking a shower? This is your opportunity to rethink towel placement.

3. If you're just planning to give your space a facelift, it's pretty straightforward. **Paint/wallpaper, make repairs/do installations.** If you are doing a complete remodel, the steps are much the same just with a longer time frame—*and in my case, a need to live elsewhere until the construction dust has been cleared out.*

4. **Heavy duty CLEAN!** Enough said. Scrub it all to its most sterile. If you're doing it, may as well do it all the way!

5. **Think logically about the things you use and where you use them to determine what goes where.** While it may seem reasonable to house your scrubbing cleanser in the shower where you use it, it's not attractive, and more importantly, I wouldn't want to mistake it for facial scrub when my eyes are closed. Having said that, it does make sense to have it housed in the bathroom to make cleaning more convenient. *Anyone who has carried a wet bucket from one room to the next, attempting to not to drip on the floor between locations, knows what I'm talking about.*

6. **Put the necessities back, NEATLY.** In the most convenient place. Straight stacks. Labels out. Fully filled containers. It may never look this good again but it will give you a starting point and a benchmark to strive for.

7. **NOW, it's time to decorate.** But remember what we discussed about keeping this space clean. This is a special environment. One that is meant to be sanitary. One that is easily filled with humidity and product particles. Don't overdress it. And PLEASE don't put everything you took out, back in, without consideration just because you have it; that will negate everything you've done.

* * *

A week later, I was back at June's condo to complete the project. The paint and wallpaper looked better than I expected. The rolling island in the center of the room had me wishing I had a bathroom this size so I could do the same. And to top it off, she had her housekeeper in just that morning, so I was truly starting with a clean slate. I was thrilled. All that was left to do was put it all together.

Now before I bog you down with the details, I want you to know upfront that everything I'm about to outline has a reason. I don't organize, or even decorate for that matter, without considering some purpose, some function, some reason. I previously had June walk me through her daily bathroom routine where we also discussed her typical cleaning, laundry, and seasonal schedule. Armed with that information, plus bags filled with new goodies, I was ready to get to work. And with June playing bridge with friends, I had the place to myself without any chance of her trying to sneak a peek before I was finished.

SHOWER OR TUB AREA

1. **Get rid of products you are not using.** We already discussed this but it always bears repeating. Get rid of any products that didn't do what they claimed (there are a few volumizing shampoos that come to my mind), or items that need to be replaced from wear (loofahs, razors), or just an overall downsizing to only the products you actually use on a regular basis.

June had done a great job of this on that first day. She streamlined her routine to include only those products she consistently used. But then she went further by requesting that a wall-mounted shower dispenser be installed. Talk about cutting down on your product clutter in the shower. I purchased a large-capacity dispenser, her son-in-law installed it, and she had already filled it with shampoo/conditioner/body wash.

The dispenser had multiple hooks to hang her loofah and shower cap for those days she had just had her hair done.

2. **Wash off the containers of drippings and crusted residue. Toss out the nickel-sized soap chips for a new bar.**

June had taken the need for this step out of the equation, but if it applies to you, please do take care of this quick and easy step to start yourself off right. And every time you clean the shower, do it again.

3. **Do you have sufficient towel hanging space for each family member? If not, add bars or hooks.** No one needs to share when it comes to towel hanging. One towel bar per user is best: no one mistakenly uses someone else's towel and each towel is given the necessary breathing room to dry before the next use. But say there are multiple people using a bathroom. I wouldn't want to be the one assigned the farthest bar away from the shower. In this case, hooks are the better alternative. Plus they offer the added bonus of not having to fold your towels "properly," and thereby alleviating the frustration of towels not being folded in precisely the same way (for appearances of course). Hooks take up less room and are more user-friendly.

In June's shower, there was a towel bar placed low on the wall opposite the showerhead, presumably for easy access for someone in a wheelchair. But without a wheelchair to block the spray, she was finding that her towel was nearly always wet. That's when I suggested she not use the bar and instead install four hooks—her bath towel, her bathrobe, and two extra hooks for when she hung her clothes on hangers near the shower to let the steam take out some of the wrinkles. This is another example of the kinds of conversations taking place with clients to learn their needs and habits.

NOTE: Speaking of shower spray, consider it when placing your products in your shower. A bar of soap in the jet stream of your showerhead will likely create a mushy mass, not only leaving you with having to clean up more often, but washing your soap away before you get a chance to use it for yourself.

VANITY AND UNDER SINK STORAGE

1. **Get rid of products you are not using.** You know the drill. If you're not using it, you need to be losing it.

June had done an amazing job of finding disposal procedures for all of her late husband's meds and medical equipment. She pitched anything of her own that was old or of no use to her. And she had also changed her habits and wasn't using as many products overall.

In order to make reaching items easier, I had purchased roll-out trays to be installed in the cabinets under her twin sinks. It was on these trays that I placed her trash can, cleaning supply bucket (explained in more detail later in this chapter) and backup family-sized supplies that were too bulky to be stored elsewhere.

2. Wash off the containers of drippings and crusted residue. Consolidate like products into one container. Separate items into categories.

June outdid herself consolidating and separating her health and beauty items. Typically, I am not a fan of buying all new organizers, opting instead to salvage and repurpose containers from around the house, but June had a clear vision for what she wanted in her new spa bathroom and I wanted to give it to her. I decided that clear-plastic zip top makeup totes would make the most sense for a number of reasons: each bag was pliable unlike a structured container so they fit together more harmoniously in her vanity drawers, likewise they were easy to remove when she used them, and they kept the items inside clean, visible, and separated by category, making it clear to determine when she needed to replenish. Each held a different category of products: makeup, facial creams and cleansers, first aid. A second drawer was filled with evenly lined backup supplies of her favorite products: soap, deodorant, body lotion. She could easily see what she needed to restock by pulling out the drawer and assessing the gaps. The rest of her day-to-day items—meds, dental care, hairbrush and accessories—were housed in her medicine cabinet for easy eye-level access on a daily basis without much bending. She asked that her hair dryer be mounted to the wall "like in a hotel" and her son-in-law had taken care of that.

3. **In the bathroom, use decor that serves a purpose beyond being pretty.** I spoke about the practicality of decorative items earlier in the chapter (rugs with non-slip backing, etc.) but let's take that a step further. In a space where utility is key, choose items that play double duty—decorative and useful.

June's theme was spa-serene. I purchased a clear lucite (again, for safety reasons, do not use glass in a bathroom) tray the width of the space between the two sinks, and three clear lucite lidded jars that were faceted to look like cut glass. I filled them with cotton rounds, cotton swabs, and in the last, June had requested it be filled with the mini hotel bar soaps from her and Paul's travels—collections in the bathroom goes against nearly everything I've discussed so far, BUT it was a lidded jar, thus keeping it dust free, and soap is on theme in a bathroom, so I agreed in order to please my client. Lastly, two matching white lucite soap dispensers (not clear, so no reason to be concerned with the color of the liquid soap inside not matching the bathroom or even each other) for each sink and a coordinating mouthwash dispenser June had purchased online. Once it was put together, it wound up being a well-appointed vanity "work" area outfitted with all easy-to-clean pieces that kept the space organized but also visually appealing.

NOTE: As tempting as it is to go to HomeGoods and buy every matching canister and cube they have to organize with, that will only add to your clutter. Determine exactly what you need and the space you have to place it in, then go and buy just that. *If you don't use cotton balls, you don't need a lidded candy jar to house them in.*

TOILET

1. **If I've said it once, I've said it too many times. Keep your toilet area well supplied with toilet paper.**

Before work began, June had a self-standing shelving unit above the toilet where she stacked towels and toilet paper. She was on the right track but...firstly, the toilet is a notoriously germy location so it's not ideal for storing your open air stack of towels and secondly, YES to the toilet paper being nearby but NOT necessarily to it being on display. There are several items on the market that will hide a stack of rolls. I removed the shelving unit and bought June a chrome (to match the handle) four-roll holder to hide out of sight behind the toilet.

NOTE: I know many of you may have a toilet brush housed in a decorative holder near your toilet. If you don't use the brush every day, it is not something that needs to be on permanent display. That goes for just about anything you use less than daily.

2. **If you need to store wipes or feminine products nearby, do it with a bit of style.**

June didn't have use for these products but I did find a white lucite lidded box that matched the soap dispensers and picked it up just in case. Had she wanted to use it, I would have filled it with a small, refillable supply of these products and placed it on the top of the toilet tank. Far more useful than a basket of shells, am I right? But at the end of the project, I hadn't found a use for it so back to the store it went.

NOTE: Word of caution. Flushable wipes should not be flushed. They WILL back up your pipes. Dispose of them in the trash. I know, gross, but I felt it had to be said to prevent you from having to hire a plumber down the road.

3. **If you'd like to dress it up, go high.** As clean as we attempt to keep this area, it is never truly free of germs. Stay away from toilet seat covers or toilet mats for this reason. But if you'd like to dress the area, a piece of artwork (many retailers carry vinyl prints that are stretched on a wood frame like real canvas artwork that you can literally sponge clean) placed high above the bowl is an easy way to add some interest.

Thankfully, the wallpaper I chose for June—an all over blues and silver geode marble look—was more than enough artwork for the area. No additional bling needed. (P.S. I loved this wallpaper so much, I bought a few rolls for myself.)

TOWELS/SUPPLIES

1. **Do you know your towel basics? Bath towel vs bath sheet? Turkish vs terry?** I'm not going to tell you that there is only one way to get dry. You have to decide the best route for yourself. Let me give you some info so you can make your own decision. Bath sheets are bigger—typically 8" bigger in both length and width than a bath towel—so they are ideal for taller or larger bathers, or anyone who just wants more. Having said that, they will require more room on bars or hooks and possibly more drying time. Terry towels have been the

gold standard for decades, but Turkish towels are filling a niche for those with limited space. They tout being super absorbent for their size and many people swear by them.

We kept it simple in June's newly designed bathroom. All fluffy white terry bath towels and hand towels, six of each. My instructions to clients are to wash used towels weekly and rotate any piles by placing the newly laundered ones on the bottom of the stack. Wash them more often if you'd like but weekly with your linens is a standard balance. And rotating the stack keeps them all in equal use. "But Bonnie, if I use them all, then I'll never have new-new towels." Then don't have six of each, have four instead, and buy new when you want new. You don't need them if you're not going to use them.

2. **How often do you go through your supplies to check for expiration dates, usefulness, amount left in the container? How often should you?**
   This is an exercise in habit building. Check your supplies as often as you make your shopping list (assuming you make a shopping list, which I highly recommend since it saves you both time and money in the grocery store) so you can replenish any low stock. Top up supplies at that time too (fill canisters of cotton balls, replace slivers of bar soap, etc.). Check expiration dates annually

on meds that you do not use regularly (OTC pain meds but also cough drops and first aid cream). Pitch and replenish as necessary. Check expiration dates on seasonal items (sunscreen, bug spray) at the start of the appropriate season. Pitch and replenish as necessary.

June had already done everything that was needed and we were starting from square one, but she had her instructions going forward and even planned to create a master inventory list to keep herself in check. "I'm getting old and forgetful. This will make things clearer on days that I'm foggy."

CLEANING & MAINTENANCE

At the end of the day, this is still a bathroom no matter how splendidly appointed. It's going to get used and that means dirty and sometimes disorganized. Keep the room in order by keeping your supplies in order.

- **Get rid of cleaning supplies you are not using.** The ones that you are not using because you don't like how they clean, or the fragrance is too strong, or they are too difficult to use.

- **Consolidate half-used bottles of the same product into one. Recycle empty containers appropriately.**

- **Wash off the containers of drippings and crusted residue.**
- **Purchase new sponges, brushes, or cut rags from old towels.**
- **Put all the products and tools in one wash bucket that easily fits under the sink.**

In my last house, I had an amazing mudroom. *I seriously still miss it.* That is where I used to store all the cleaning supplies for the entire house. One utilitarian location seemed the most obviously organized way to store them, right? That was until years later, after working with this system for well over a decade, I wondered why I had set up this unnecessary and inefficient first step. Why hadn't I put the cleaning supplies where they would be used instead of having to transport them each time I cleaned?

Some of you are probably thinking, "duh, you didn't know that already?" but this is where I laughingly admit, as much as I'd like to think I'm an all-knowing organizing deity standing atop a Jenga stack of bar soap, wielding my toilet brush scepter, I'm not. Even I have to figure out a thing or two by trial and error. Luckily as a home organizer, I get a lot of opportunities for correction and tweaking the system. If I can show even a few of you how to skip some of the side steps I took to get to a more efficient way of doing things, it will all be worth it to admit I don't always get it right the first time.

With that said, the new system in my own house and those of my clients is to **streamline cleaning products and put them in the space where you will use them, out of sight of course.** That way everything is right where you need it when you need it.

Then create a cleaning calendar and stick to it. If you have a housekeeper, they are already on a schedule, but if you are cleaning for yourself, **pick a day.** For whatever reason, I like Mondays. This is my routine:

1. **Pull out the cleaning supplies. Put cleaning products on everything. Clean off everything in the same order I covered them in products. Then put supplies back.**

2. **Rag dust wall art and decorative items.**

3. **Vacuum the mats and floor (best at getting up dust and hair) then steam clean the floor (best for getting up everything else).**

4. **Collect the towels off bars and hooks and throw them in the laundry (Monday is also laundry day).**

5. **Fill up any supplies that need a top off or replacement. Make a quick note of anything to buy the next time I go grocery shopping (which is Wednesdays).**

6. Tie up the trash and reline the can.

By doing this every week, the bathroom never gets beyond control and stays sufficiently sanitary. I typically use one bath towel per week except when I may be taking multiple showers a day. Same goes for hand towels (like June, I use loofahs so no washcloths). This keeps laundering to a reasonable amount as well. Of course, if your household has more people using a bathroom, this may need to be done twice a week to maintain cleanliness and appearance. Same applies to washing the towels more than once a week so you're not putting undue stress on your washing machine and dryer by doing them all at once. Plus keep it neat daily by wiping away all visible splashes, suds, and toothpaste blobs while they are still wet and easy to remove. And put a quick shine on the faucet too. Just a tissue will do the trick. It makes a big difference.

DECOR JUST FOR JUNE

June had been through a lot. Watching her husband, whom she often referred to as her "soulmate," decline quickly in his final years, was emotionally difficult as well as physically exhausting. Over the course of their 23-year marriage (it was the second marriage for both of them), they had traveled extensively through Europe. Unfortunately, soon after he retired, his condition became their only focus and money for medical expenses ate into their plans for more travel.

Most of their days were spent within their four walls of their condo, which provided access to the services he required. June did the best she could given that she was struggling with her own issues of depression. She fought a losing battle when it came to her surroundings, what with Paul's medical equipment and mobility constraints. Knowing too that he was nearing the end of his life, she gave in to his decorating tastes regardless of how she felt about them. The truth was, they played further into her feelings of sadness over how she and Paul were spending his final days. She needed this current change more than she realized. I was happy to help her see her vision come to light.

With all that in mind, I wanted her primary bathroom to be a showstopper. Of the options I presented her with that day at the salon, June had chosen a 10' square rug with an abstract floral pattern in turquoise and neutrals that coordinated beautifully with the wallpaper. I positioned it in the middle of the room where it took up the majority of the open floor space—not an easy feat with a bathroom this spacious. I rolledthe newly painted cart into the very center of the rug. The cart had two shelves below the top surface giving me ample room to stack her folded towels on the center shelf, line scented candles (her favorite vanilla) on the bottom shelf, and display a bouquet of white hydrangeas in a large turquoise glazed pot I found in another room. *I explained to her later that these were just grocery store flowers and for*

$7.99 they were an easy pick up item every other week to keep her in fresh supply.

I stepped out of the bathroom and closed the door behind me. I needed to clear my head to see the space with fresh eyes. After a quick heat-up to my ice cold coffee, I walked back into the room and "used" it.

- I opened drawers and cabinets determining if the items inside were clearly visible and easy to reach, if bath mats were positioned in line with using the sink, if soap dispensers were user-friendly—I did have to add flat rubber feet to the bottom of each so they did not shift when pumped.
- I checked the toilet area to see if it was well-stocked with toilet paper.
- Moving onto the shower area, the dispensers were all filled with shampoo, conditioner, and body wash. A new loofah hung on the hook. A fresh towel and her newly purchased terry bathrobe hung on the two hooks closest to the shower.
- I checked that the rug was secure, and for safety purposes also added flat rubber feet to the bottom of the flower-filled pottery on top of the cart.

The room was organized, user-friendly, and well-appointed. And yes, it did have the spa-like qualities I envisioned for her. I was so pleased with how it turned out. And I was very excited for June to see her new space. I had about ten more minutes before she was due back, so I lit some of her new candles and dimmed the lights. Remember the bonus item I mentioned earlier? It was a dimmer switch on her overhead lights to complete the full spa treatment! I closed the bathroom door and waited for her in the living room.

"Hi! I'm so excited to see what you've done," she said as she practically bounded into the room. "And I'm excited for you to see it," I replied.

When we got to the closed door she looked at me and smiled. I smiled back. "Go ahead and open the door to your new bathroom." She opened the door and stood in silence just scanning the room, taking in every detail. For a moment I thought she was unhappy with the results since the pause was longer than I expected, but it was at that moment that she put her hand over her mouth and her eyes welled up with tears.

"I can't believe this is mine. It's perfect."

I just smiled and put my arm around her shoulders.

"I may never leave," she said with a devilish grin. "Is it weird that I want to take a shower in the middle of the day?"

"Not at all. In fact, I'm going to leave you to enjoy it."

"Let me pay you first! My goodness, you deserve that!" June wrote me my final check, we hugged, and I grabbed my bag. Then she said, "I'm going to call you next week. I want to do my bedroom next."

"You got it. Enjoy your spa afternoon."

* * *

June and I worked together on several more projects over the next few years. We had lost touch after the projects were completed but her daughter and son-in-law called me to tell me of her passing. They also asked if I would come back to stage the condo for sale. I was surprised and pleased to see the bathroom was in nearly the same condition as that day she saw it for the first time. June had embraced the new routines to support her new organized and user-friendly life.

"Mom always loved this room best! She called it her oasis," her daughter told me. The thought of that made me smile through my tearing eyes.

2

And If You Look Left, You'll See the Formal Living Room & Dining Room

I have a love/hate relationship with the formal rooms in most homes. On the one hand, they go against everything I stand for: furniture and items rarely used, in a space reserved for people who don't usually live there. On the other hand, generally speaking these rooms are always neat because they don't get much use. And I do so love for things to be neat.

Since moving, I no longer have a formal living room or dining room in my house. I don't miss them, usually. But I do miss the feeling of sneaking off to them whenever the rest of my home felt in disarray. I could always count on them to be the peaceful picture of order, while I'd plot my attack on the family-made mess one room over. However, I'm happy to see that the concept of formal living and dining rooms have ever so slightly gone out of fashion to make room for open-concept family living. It just makes sense. After all, we no more need these rooms in our homes than we do receiving rooms or sitting rooms.

"But Bonnie, then my whole house will be just one big playground! I need something nice meant for grown-ups. And what about when we have company? I don't want them to have to sit in the chaos."

I get it. I do. I'm just, as always, offering an alternative notion to your present situation based on my mantra of using and loving what you have, instead of just having it. So indulge me. When was the last time you sat in your living room?

PRACTICALITY. By definition, formal rooms are not practical, but let me offer some food for thought. *But no actual food in the living room, please.*

- If this were a book written in the 60s, it might be a point of practicality to suggest plastic slipcovers. But it's not, and I won't. EVER! Even as I stand firmly on the idea of keeping things neat and clean, I am opposed to preserving things. You don't live in a museum. *What were those plastic slipcovers meant to do? To prevent spill stains from your whiskey sour? To keep out the smell of stale Lucky Strikes?*

- My only word of advice here is less is more when it comes to decorating these spaces. There is going to be dust. *And now that I think about it, dog hair, because my dogs were really the only ones who have ever used the living room on a regular basis. It had good sun!*

If you are in the habit of not using your formal rooms with the idea of keeping them neat, I'm going to suggest you start using them, every day, in some way. Read. Have a cup of coffee. Chat with a friend there instead of at the kitchen table. Set up your laptop and work, *in the sun, next to the dog.* But use it. It's yours. You've worked hard to accumulate the things that are there, probably fairly expensive things. Don't save it for company. Be practical about your space and give it purpose.

EFFICIENCY. Efficiency is not the first thing one might consider when thinking about formal living spaces. I mean, if they don't get used all that much, how efficient do they need to be? I say, every space that people occupy must "work."

- Can you push your chairs back from the dining table without hitting the walls or other pieces of furniture?
- Is there enough space to walk behind a dining chair if someone is sitting in it?

- Can you walk the entire circumference of your table and chairs with and without guests?
- When you pull the dining chairs out to sit, are the back legs off the rug? Is there a rug? Is it a sufficient size in proportion to the table and chairs?
- Is your buffet cluttered with items that prevent you from using it to serve food?
- Does your china cabinet have enough space inside to hold all your china, service pieces, silverware, crystal glassware, etc.?
- Are your formal linens (tablecloths, runners, napkins) housed in the dining room? What about a backstock of candle tapers and long lighter or matches?
- And in the living room, is your furniture set up for ease of sitting and reaching for drinks off the coffee table or side tables?
- Do you have to maneuver around pieces of furniture to get to a place on the couch, loveseat, settee, arm chair?
- And what about the piano, if you have one? Is it placed against an interior wall as recommended?

See what I mean? *My brain can turn almost anything into an opportunity for efficiency.*

ROUTINE. How do you plan on maintaining this newly organized and decorated space?

- How often will you dust, vacuum, condition the wood?
- How often will you rotate your oriental rugs or have the upholstery and draperies steam cleaned?
- Are you on a maintenance schedule with your piano tuner, clock oilings, wallpaper hanger and painter?
- And what about polishing that silver? Or cleaning the chandelier?

Who knew so much work went into rooms you rarely use?

DECOR. This is really what these rooms are all about, right? They are the interior decorating equivalent of getting dressed up in full makeup and heels to attend an event. Not an everyday occurrence; only for special occasions. That concept kinda bothers me, I'm not gonna lie. Because in treating these rooms this way there is a whole list of decor faux pas well-intentioned home dwellers make:

- Overdressing: Coco Chanel has been credited with saying "once you've dressed, and before

you leave the house, look in the mirror and take at least one thing off." This applies to your home as well. But my own quote would go something like "once you've decorated, remove anything you don't want to keep clean." Objets d'art, framed photos, and books are the things that come to mind for me.
- Oversized pieces with multiple diminutive pieces: That goes for any room in your house, but with a room that doesn't get much use, you run the risk of it looking more like storage space than a planned design when you have an hodgepodge of sizes. It's as bad as a mixed bag of designs/periods. And petite furnishings that can't be used because they are too fragile and small need to go. *I sound like a skipping record; if you can't use it, lose it.*
- Poor lighting. Heavy window treatments. Mis-sized area rugs. I don't think this needs much explanation.
- Use your walls. Whether that means art or wallpaper, use your underused wall space to raise your eye and clear your surfaces. *Yes, it all still needs to be dusted but at least it's not taking up usable tabletops.*

I've given a good amount of thought to the concept of formal rooms and here is what I'd like to see going forward in the family home. **I'd like to see these areas**

turned into usable, purposeful, family-friendly but not necessarily children-centered spaces. Think living-room-as-study rather than a sitting room only to host guests. Think of the dining room as an every Sunday brunch table, instead of, inexplicably, as a stacking spot for everything from paperwork to puzzles—*it's that big table, I kind of get it, but that doesn't make it right.*

My version of these rooms is a multitasking space that can be converted for several situations INCLUDING formal. A working area or office, a reading nook, a family gaming space, all which can be tidied easily and methodically and yet not in a throw-all-the-pieces-in-a-drawer sort of way. A place that may not get the day-to-day use, but gets occupied more than just holidays and family functions.

* * *

My client Tara was the first one to take me up on this new concept. She and her six-year-old daughter Saoirse had just moved to Maryland from South Carolina. She had taken a new job with the Justice Department which started almost immediately. The multistate move was rushed and barely left time to enroll her daughter in school, much less settle in and decorate. I had been marketing to new homeowners in her neighborhood and it was one of my cards that prompted her to call me with the somewhat unusual request of unpacking and setting up her house. Usually my work is about fixing what is already there, not building it from the ground up. But it was an exciting proposition.

Tara had bought a sun-filled raised ranch on a cherry tree lined street in College Park, MD. The main level of the house had three bedrooms, two baths, living room, dining room, and eat-in kitchen. The bottom level was unfinished, but she planned to convert it into a one-bedroom apartment in the hopes of a rental income. When I arrived for our meeting, her daughter was playing in the driveway, drawing with colored chalk. "Are you the lady who is going to fix our house?" Saoirse said as I was exiting the car.

"Yes, I am."

"Good. Mama can't find my sparkly shoes. And I really want a hanging chair in my room."

I laughed. "Okay, I like that you know what you want. I'll talk to your mom about it and we'll see what we can do." I smiled at her and walked up the path to the front porch.

Tara was already opening the door as I got near and had me follow her into the house.

"Thank God you are here. I'm losing my head. I heard Saoirse tell you about the chair. Good Lord she saw it on an HGTV program and now she won't let up about it. Can I get you an iced tea?"

Tara was southern hospitality personified. The pitcher of tea and homemade ginger peach scones were giving me ideas galore for this lovely woman and her daughter as they began their new life. We chatted for a few hours while we toured her home and she told me about herself.

The house she left in South Carolina was bigger and had both a formal living and dining room, but her money didn't go as far in Maryland. While she technically had these rooms in this house, she also needed spaces that were more livable. That's when I presented her with my idea and she ate it up with a spoon. Before I left, *with a container full of scones,* I gave her just a bit of homework to manage before I came back in a few days.

"You've got the next few days to get to this list, right?" I asked, taking the last swig of my iced tea.

"Yes, ma'am. Knowing you've got the rest makes what I have to do easy," Tara replied with a wink as she reached out for the scrawled **to-do list** I slid to her across the table.

- **Move boxes to the correct rooms** or at least as best as you can.
- **Same with furniture** if it's not already there.
- ***Please leave me some more scones.***

And that was it! Tara needed an office space for days she worked from home. Her hobbies were sewing, reading, and wine. Saoirse loved to play with dolls and her dollhouse along with arts and crafts.

Mother and daughter were very close and Tara wanted to cultivate that by adding a play area to the space so Saoirse wouldn't be playing alone in her room. And Saoirse had given me her own list, *complete with stickers.* It was certainly a lot to consider for one space but it was completely doable given we were literally starting from scratch.

* * *

You might be wondering how I approach a job like this. Why don't I **take you through my process** so you can do the same for yourself in your own home? I always start the same way by asking the questions, **"What is the purpose of this space and how can I make it functional?"** Making beautiful rooms always comes last in my mind. *A beautiful room with no purpose that can't be used is called an art installation and the average family home doesn't have any need for that.*

1. **Ask yourself what you'd like the room to serve as; what is its purpose?** You can literally make any room, with the exception of the bathroom or kitchen, into anything you want it to be. Just because the original blueprints for the house read LIVING ROOM doesn't mean you have to make it so. *I've been in quite a few homes with dining rooms turned into bedrooms for ailing elderly family members;*

it's your house so use the space to suit you and your family.

2. Now that you know what you'd like it to be, **how do you create a space that can be all those things AND work in such a way that it stays orderly and organized?** The answer is functional furnishings, visual room dividers, and creative storage. *Of course, just having less stuff works too.* As for functionality, that Louis XIV settee is really only big enough for one adult and a preschooler. Maybe it's not the best option for a family of four. Neither is that overstuffed velour eight-piece sectional sofa with the cup holders built in if you have to walk across the seat cushions to get to the other end because it takes up all the floor space.

3. **Create your areas based on the room's environment.** If your room gets direct sunlight, just know that by placing upholstered pieces near windows, they will fade. If the door from one room to the next swings into an item you've placed in its path, move that item or remove the door. Also, be aware of heating/AC vents, any integrated lighting, and outlets and switches already in the room. *You can't have a reading nook without an outlet for a lamp nearby.*

4. **Devise a plan for furniture placement.** Think about the walking path through a room; you shouldn't have to snake around furniture. If your room is going to play double or triple duty as several spaces, consider visual cues to separate them like rugs, consoles, even potted plants. Think about ease of use. Can you access every seat in a space or do you need to maneuver around something to sit? If that's the case, adjust accordingly and that may mean removing it altogether. Lastly, don't block those vents. *The back of your curio cabinet doesn't need the air conditioning.*

5. **Listen to your heart when it comes to your personal tastes.** Disregard what is "in" at the moment or even what is out of fashion. This is your home. It should be a reflection of you and your family before all else. The interior designer Nate Berkus is credited with saying "Your home should tell the story of who you are and be a collection of what you love." *I agree.*

* * *

The floor plan of Tara's home was not unlike others built during the 1970s. Upon entering the front door, there was a small foyer area which led into the living room that extended straight to the back of the house. The only cue that these were two separate spaces was the flooring, which in the foyer was slate and in the living room was hardwood. Turning right off the foyer was the eat-in area of the kitchen, behind which was the cooking area. Both beyond the kitchen and off to the right of the living room at the back of the house was the dining room. And both the living room and dining room had sliding glass doors that lead to the patio and a walled garden. It was a lovely space that had ample afternoon light. But it was the morning light, casting shadows across the floor from the swaying cherry trees outside the kitchen window that made me feel a connection to Tara and her daughter; it was in that moment of warm meditative serenity that it felt like everything was going to be alright for all of us. My daughter and I were on a similar adventure—newly separated, new school, starting my own business—and I wanted to give these southern belles the fresh start I had begun for myself.

Tara had left me the keys and I let myself in. She had done all her homework, including leaving me a batch of blueberry scones dipped in white chocolate. *No need to go out for lunch now.* If you recall, Tara's list of wishes for her living room and dining room were a work area, possibly a hobby area, bar area, play area, and smaller traditional living room. My grand ideas for this space were a bit out-of-the-box but she gave me the green light to do anything with hopeful trepidation.

First thing I did was throw out the decades-old intended reasons for these rooms and **reassigned all the furniture.**

- **Her dining room would become her daughter's playroom.** I made the decision to move her whitewashed French Provincial dining room table and chairs to the kitchen. I couldn't see leaving such a beautiful collection of furniture in a nonessential room when both the furniture and the room could be put to better use. The kitchen window seat bench would make the slight formality of the table more homey and thus make the transition of these pieces near seamless. Plus, since she had just reupholstered the bench cushion and had tons of fabric leftover, I could reupholster the chair seats to match. This switch was already proving to be a huge improvement.

    With the dining room empty, I moved all the boxes marked toys, plus Saoirse's dollhouse into what was now the playroom. I would deal with the organization of that space later. I had more pressing tasks.

- **The rear of the living room, closest to the playroom and patio, would become Tara's office/hobby/bar area.** This proximity provided Tara with the "parallel play" scenario she wanted with

Saoirse. I moved the former kitchen table to this space to become her new desk/workstation and added both armchairs from the old dining set to become her desk chair and guest chair which sat across from each other. The table was natural pine, but I preferred the whitewashed tone of the chairs, so I texted Tara requesting the option to stain it to match. She agreed, and I added that to my to-do list.

- It was at this point that I took a **walk through the house, shopping from Tara's belongings** to make this new space cohesive. In Saoirse's room, I found a padded muslin-covered bench seat with a hinged lid that opened to storage. And it was only partially filled with toys. *Ding! Ding!* I had found my visual room divider between the playroom and her new office space. I couldn't wait to slide it into place. It was better than expected: room divider, toy storage, and extra seating in one. And just as important, its width left sufficient space to move between the two rooms. *Yay!*

- **The living area of the living room was next.** Tara had such lovely southern traditional furniture. A beautiful butter-yellow sofa and loveseat, an oriental rug in greens and yellows, a wing chair upholstered in a pastel flame stitch fabric, and a coffee table and two end tables in high-gloss black, hand painted with magnolias. I maneuvered the sofa into place against the left wall that ran the length of the room and about four feet from where the hardwood met the slate floor of the foyer. I laid the rug in front of the sofa and pushed the loveseat to the far end of the rug facing the front door. With the loveseat in this position, an area divider was created between the living room and the office space. Then it took no thought at all to place the accent tables in their typical homes.

- **Time for another shopping trip around the house.** This time for lamps and possibly a console table *hopefully with wine bottle storage.* In my search, however, I discovered something just as good. Art! Lots of ornate gold-framed art pieces ranging in size from 3" square to 3'x5' horizontal. The complete vision for the living area came into focus and it included a gallery wall. *I was buzzing! Time for a quick coffee break to think it all through and then push forward. I wanted the bulk of this space complete before Tara and Saoirse got home.*

NOTE: I'm not sure if this qualifies as a "life hack" but it certainly does solve a myriad of issues. Before you buy new, often meaningless mass-produced objects, and add to your pile of possessions, **shop from your stock.** Give new purpose to something you already own. All too often we get tied to the notion that something can only ever have one given meaning and it must conform to these rigid interior decorating and design principles. I don't believe there are any rules in good design other than to ask "does it work for you?" *Now, I personally don't think everything has a place in your home. If I did, I wouldn't have spent my entire last book explaining how to get rid of stuff. But I don't live in your house either, so if it works, and I mean actually works, not "I can't part with it so I'll make it work," go for it!* This concept comes up frequently in my work, most often as I attempt to find things in a client's home to solve an organizing need and I am generally against store-bought organizers which create more clutter than streamline it. You will find furnishings in places they were not intended, in nearly all of my projects. Dressers for filing cabinets, children's play tables as indoor gardens, tablecloths for curtains, and in this case, a bookcase as a wine bar.

My signature suggestion came about by surprise. The unfinished lower level was a goldmine. Tara said it was an assortment of items she packed but planned to get rid of and things the previous owners left behind. She hadn't really given much thought to them, planning instead to just put them out at the curb on the next junk day. But once I was down there, I told her to hold off until we finished the house. There might be treasures.

What I found was a 3-shelf bookcase only about two feet wide. It was in rough shape but it was solid wood and had an attractive design so I thought it could be used for a project with some shining up. Then I found a large cutting board slightly bigger than the top of the bookcase and the idea came to light.

I somehow managed to get it upstairs by laying it on a sheet and pushing it some of the way. I put it against the wall between the desk and the loveseat. It fit the space perfectly. I had the bar! And I figured if I couldn't come up with how to put it together, I could always use the bookcase as a filing system for Tara's paperwork. First things first, I ran to the kitchen for a bottle of wine, ran back to the bookcase and placed it on a shelf lying down. Yes! Near perfect! Just a bit of the neck of the bottle extended past the shelf.

Now for the cutting board. I placed it on top of the bookshelf and checked for stability. It was solidly in place. Even still, I planned to attach it somehow to keep it that way. But I was certain this would be Tara's new wine bar, and added its creation to my to-do list along with reupholstering the new kitchen chairs and staining the new workstation desk. Plenty of room for wine bottles, glasses, and tools. Plus when she entertained, easy access for her guests to refill as well.

I looked around the room and it was really all coming

together. I had an hour before Tara and Saoirse would be home. Just enough time to put boxes in the proper areas and hang two paintings to show what would become the gallery wall. One painting Tara had mentioned was her favorite, and the other was painted by Saoirse. *Making a space personal makes a huge impact on my clients. I always want them to feel that a room is theirs and not mine. I want them to feel like this is who they were all along, they just weren't sure how to get there.*

When they walked in the front door, I immediately said, "It's not done yet, so please reserve judgment for when it's all put together." Tara replied, "Are you kidding me, I thought you were just coming up with a plan today. This looks near finished!" Saoirse walked wide-eyed through the living room, then let out a little shriek when she saw all her toys in her new playroom. "Mama look! Ahhh!" as she dove into the basket of dolls on the floor and started playing. *Little does she know the magic that's in store for her once I actually do something with her playroom.*

I walked Tara through the space explaining what I had done and what I still planned to do. Then I said I'd be back in the morning and excused myself for the day so they could take it all in.

* * *

Time for a quick recap of what I did and what you can do in any space in your house.

1. **Determine the uses for all your spaces in a given room and move the furniture.** Don't try to force all of it. *Both of Tara's dining room armchairs were now part of the office space, not the eat-in kitchen area. They didn't fit and weren't necessary since she had a window seat bench. They were not only needed but completely useful as a desk chair and guest chair.*

2. As you move things, **determine what, if any, items will be repurposed and/or upcycled.** Even though you are mixing sets, that doesn't automatically mean it will look like a mishmash. Alter items just enough to give everything in a room continuity. I hasten to add, however, not to push the envelope too far and attempt to make everything matchy matchy, *you know I'm not a fan.* While it seems like painting all your furniture the same color would automatically make it look cohesive, nothing makes a space more glaringly misfit-esque than to color wash everything.

3. **Shop your stock.** These days, it's honestly my favorite way to shop. And if you have a group of like-minded people, you can **swap your stock too.** *The town of Amherst, MA where I live has a strong recycling spirit and the Buy Nothing Facebook page is always filled with*

amazing items people are just giving away. Don't turn your nose down at these gifts. Take advantage of them and then make them your own.

4. There is nothing that dictates you must use your furniture for its original purpose. **Give your things a new reason to be in your home other than taking up space.** Have no need for those bedside tables? Paint them a fun color, put them side by side or on top of one another, and turn them into storage for kids' craft supplies. Useful is always better than useless. *And if it's useless, it need not take up space in your home. Move it along.*

* * *

For the next two and a half days, the rest of this multiroom redesign wrapped up without a snag.

- **I prioritized the upcycling projects** by sanding the soon-to-be wine bar and workstation, then applying a coat of stain which would take a full 24 hours to dry between coats. I had picked up a quart of "pickled oak" wood stain to give these pieces a complementary shade between the natural wood and the distressed whitewash of the former dining armchairs. It was a gamble but I was happy with how it came out. Worst case scenario, I'd have to run out for paint.

- **I reupholstered the dining chairs** with what was left of the bench fabric. *If you plan to do this kind of upholstery project regularly, it's worth purchasing an electric staple gun. It makes the process incredibly fast and easy.*

- I moved onto **hanging the gallery wall.** *There are dozens of ways to do this and, to be completely honest, I'm probably not the best person to ask because I generally wing it. I hang something, stand back, hang something else, stand back; it's an organic process that takes a good amount of time.* My one piece of advice, beyond watching videos on "how to hang a gallery wall" which is a must, is to use all the same hardware whether you choose picture hangers or just plain nails. Being consistent will mean not having to make measurement adjustments for different sizes and shapes of hooks.

- Time to dive into **organizing Saoirse's playroom.** I had very little in the way of furniture to work with, but I knew that Tara's intention was for Saoirse to play in this room as opposed to her bedroom. With this in mind, I moved the majority of the toys from her room into this space, along with any toy bins/baskets I could find and a four-box cubby unit. I still had the four kitchen chairs left over from the furniture switch. I decided to use them to create a fort thingy. I placed them in a square with the seats facing each other and covered the whole thing with white netting I found in Tara's sewing stuff. *I crossed my fingers she didn't need it for anything because I had a feeling Saoirse was going to go insane for this.* (As for the nuts and bolts of organizing a playroom, I will get into that in Chapter 6.)

- Onto **organizing Tara's work area.** Staining furniture always delays progress, but I used that time to work out the logistics of lamps and decor. Again, I shopped from around the house and back in the basement where I found some items I thought I could repurpose as organizers.

* * *

CLEANING & MAINTENANCE

Unlike the serious sanitary cleaning that goes into a bathroom or kitchen, keeping the living areas of your home clean really comes down to getting in the habit of keeping it neat as you use it.

- **ALWAYS, put things away.** Which also means that everything in your home has a home. *So, when you are finished with that cup of coffee, it doesn't stay on the coffee table. Bring it into the kitchen.*

- Dust happens. Pet hair happens. **Make it part of your regular routine to dust and vacuum every or every other week.** Just a quick feather dusting and vacuuming of all walkways is all that is required. Save the heavy duty moving of furniture and polishing of wood for monthly or even quarterly cleanings...*or shh, even yearly if you can get away with it.* Oh, don't forget to vacuum any window treatments; *the dust that collects in those things is surprisingly thick.*

- Think quick when it comes to mishaps. **Treat stains as soon as they happen.**

- I mentioned earlier in the chapter that there is **maintenance on such things as your piano or grandfather clock.** Here's the thing. You don't have to! But know that if things start to perform less than efficiently, the fix MAY require a bit more effort if there have not been regular checkups. *If you've got a budding virtuoso in the house, then yes, consider annually tuning your piano to keep it and them in perfect harmony.*

- **Rotate your fabrics** to prevent, or at least evenly distribute, fading from the sun. Move upholstered furniture, swap out throw pillows, or just be aware that this is going to happen and let it be the natural progression of the pieces. *I have a few pieces that are bleached white on the back and I like to think of it as the history of the piece.*

- Lastly, some decorating tidbits: set your decorative items and keep it that way. **If you add, subtract.** New photos of the family? Swap out a photo already in a frame instead of adding another framed photo. Why?

    Because adding means more to maintain, and that leaves the door open to clutter, and clutter becomes disorderly quickly, which is a slippery slope to full-on disorganized nightmare, and next thing you know, you're paying someone like me to come in to fix it all because you "needed" another photo of your dog on the mantle in a room, where I will have to remind you, only the dog goes anyway.

    Whew! Rant over. Notice, however, that I did not put a restriction on the number of decorative items you could display in the first place. <wink>

DECOR JUST FOR TARA & SAOIRSE

I remember it was a Friday. I was heading out of state for the weekend so I would be in Tara's house only half the day to make the final adjustments. I, of course, had many more weeks ahead in this house to unpack and set up, but I was nearly done with this space. I walked in the front door attempting to see a room I had been ensconced in for the last week, with fresh eyes. Again, as it had been that first morning, the shadows of the cherry tree were dancing across the floor and it made me so happy. I hoped that walking into their house at the end of each day had the same effect on Tara and Saoirse.

But once in the room I felt a block. My eyes darted back and forth throughout the room, moving furniture in my mind like mental chess pieces. There was something that was not right and it made me feel the slightest bit trapped instead of welcome. I stepped forward crossing from the foyer into the living room and that's when it hit me. The loveseat that was making the long-established L-shape conversation triangle (it's a decorating principle) was blocking most of the natural light from the back of the house. It also prevented having a visual on the new workstation. It had to be changed because while Tara may not have been able to articulate the problem, she would certainly feel it. *It was making me physically uncomfortable but I'm a bit weird that way.*

The adjustments wouldn't be terribly difficult but this was not what I had planned for this morning. Nonetheless, I put down my things and got started. The pathway from the front door to the back of the house ran down the right wall, which you'll remember

I made into a gallery wall. I would have to raise a few of the frames or shuffle them around but it would open the space to slide the loveseat under the gallery wall. Unfortunately, this also meant that I would be taking up the pathway space to the back of the room. In turn, the rug would have to be adjusted so anyone walking through did not have one foot on a rug and one foot on the floor. I shifted the rug not just in front of the long sofa, but under it, clearing just enough of the wood floor to create a more distinct walkway.

Was that really all it took? I stepped out of the house and walked back in. *Yup! That was it!* With the loveseat out of the way, I could see clear out the back sliding glass door to the patio, and it was freeing. Plus, it opened up the visual on the new workstation, *which turned out lovely, practical, and neat as a pin if I do say so myself.* It felt really beautiful and pristine and yet lived-in and enjoyed at the same time. I couldn't wait for Tara's reaction. She already loved the dining table in the kitchen, especially with the new upholstery. She was also finding it easy to work from home with her new workstation. Saoirse was gaga for her playroom! And mother and daughter could spend happy hours together, and together but separate, just as Tara had asked for at the start. This project was joyful on so many levels.

Tara called me that evening. "Girl, what did you do? The room looks bigger and brighter." She hadn't even noticed I moved things around but she noticed that it felt better. That's when I know I've done my job well.

3

Please Remove Your Shoes

If I could grant three wishes to anyone and everyone, those wishes would be: a life that makes you happy, a passion that drives you onward, and a mudroom in every home. Truth! To know the magic of a mudroom is to experience the perfect staging area to prepare for the comings and goings to the outside world. Where coats are buttoned, car keys are grabbed, and pets lay patiently waiting for the return of their people at the end of the day. A life where family commitments, schedules, and routines—and the dance it takes to navigate them all—converge. Part laundry, part pet room, part workshop, part coatroom, it is in my humble opinion the true "heart of the home." And while other people dream of the perfect pantry or oversized walk-in closet, I could spend hours pouring over glossy photos of multitasking mudrooms complete with actual mud.

What I think I love most about a mudroom is that it is organization, efficiency, and purpose in one need-based package. The more I wax poetic, the more the mudroom becomes a metaphor for all beginnings and endings of daily life and the epitome of family. In my last home, I had a spacious and oh-so-organized mudroom. Friends and family never entered through the front door. If you were welcome in our home, you walked in through the garage and directly into the mudroom. *Knocking optional; calling out "Hello!" a given.* A room that for 20 years, hosted piles of kids' shoes during afterschool playdates, where sleeping dogs curled up on the floor in the morning sun surrounded by laundry and grocery bags, where warm greetings as well as tough conversations followed by slamming doors, took place. *Family is not all fun and games, sometimes it gets heated. But the mudroom was a quick escape out of the house and away from the tension.*

But not everyone has the privilege of such a space in their home. That doesn't mean you can't carve out a nook to serve that purpose. Any spare area near the most commonly used exit/entrance in your home will do, even, as you will see, if you have next to no space at all.

PRACTICALITY. Mudroom = practicality. Period. You need it even if you don't take your shoes off in your house. You need a place for coats, library books that need to be returned, and reusable grocery bags that need to go back in the car or you'll forget them the next time you shop. Need. Need. Need. And what do you need to make it work? Storage! Easy access, user-friendly, low-maintenance storage.

- Heavy iron hooks. Attached to the wall studs or to a 2"x4" that is attached to the studs. These hooks need to take weight. Don't leave that kind of pressure to drywall anchors.
- Shoe storage. Whether that is a shoe rack or an over door shoe organizer or a basket in an under bench cubby, you need a place to line up shoes to keep them paired. Boot trays are a must for rain, mud, and snow.
- Accessory storage. For hats, gloves, earmuffs. For phone chargers, school supplies, errant car items.
- Wardrobe or other hanging space. Shelves. Some kind of closed cabinets. A junk drawer or two. Depending on your goal for your space, not to mention the size of your space, not all these things are necessary but if you have the room, go for it.

NOTE: Purchase or create organizers based on your needs. Do not purchase or create organizers and then try to make your stuff and lifestyle conform to them. *It DOES NOT WORK that way.* And very quickly, you will find that your well-appointed mudroom full of organizing "essentials" doesn't keep you organized.

- Easy-to-clean flooring. From slate and ceramic tiling to hardwood and laminate to indoor/outdoor carpet. It all works depending on the debris that comes in your home and how much effort you want to put into cleaning it.
- And lastly, in a perfect world, a washer and dryer and a big utility sink to complete the practicality of this essential space.

EFFICIENCY. A place for everything and everything in its place, with a focus on lifestyle. What would a room designed for work be like without organizing systems in place and the routines and habits to keep them running? The answer is a hot mess. Beyond the cubicles and cubbies is the all-important fact that the systems must be user-friendly for your particular family members. Not all organizational setups are equal—*says the 5' tall home organizer who begs you to consider the height of the people who live in your house.*

- Do you have littles? No time like the present to teach them how to clean up after themselves. But making it too difficult will result in meltdowns and rebellion. Don't require them to hang their coats on a hanger and place it on a

Please Remove Your Shoes

bar high above their head. Give them a hook they can reach. Same with shoes. Lined up or in little cubbies can be a step too many when they have snacks on the brain. Let them throw their shoes in a basket (one per kid; maybe even let them decorate their own). This gets the shoes out of the way, still teaches them a lesson of how to keep things neat, and on a side note, when the remains of the playground come off their shoes, it's easier to knock a basket outside to clean it than to have to take a sponge to a cubby.

- Are you using your space for pets? Keep food near the bowls so there is not needless walking to and fro with spillable items. Leash and baggies near the door for walks with a backup supply nearby. Comfy bed or crate for when you are out of the house. Most dogs stay near the door you left out of instinct. May as well make it nice for them while you're gone.

- Is this your laundry space as well? I can't begin to explain the joy of coming in from gardening, wet with sweat and soil, and immediately throwing those filthy clothes in the washer without even entering the rest of the house. I should probably mention it's a good idea to keep a stack of beach towels nearby if this practice of stripping down is something you do on the regular. *Or, feel free to run through your house to the shower au naturel, your choice.*

- Does this area house cleaning equipment, arts and crafts supplies, table linens, or outdoor and beach items? It could if you want it to but remember, user-friendly is the goal to keeping a working room neat. *Again, my last house's mudroom held all of these plus all the above. Can you tell I miss it?*

ROUTINE. For a room with practicality and efficiency as its purpose, there is only one way to keep it neat. Habits built on routine.

- If your mudroom space is set up appropriately, there should be little reason it falls out of order. Shoes go where shoes go. Coats go where coats go. Etc.
- It should be so effortless as to be immediately self-explanatory upon seeing the space, where everything goes. Shoes go where the shoes are. Coats go where the coats are. Etc.
- Given the prior knowledge for every possible use in this area, there should be a procedure for all of them. Shoes go...*you know where I'm going with this.*

- And following through on these new systems makes the mudroom the well-oiled machine it was created to be.

DECOR. Even the most pragmatic of places can be dressed up with purpose.

- Bulletin boards, white boards, calendars, hanging folder pockets all in line with keeping the family schedules humming along.
- Wall mirror for that last check before heading out into the world.
- Bowls, clear lidded jars, containers of some sort to house the articles of life from car keys to crayons.
- Washable, absorbent area rugs.
- Plexiglass and wood frames for kids' art if you want to get fancy.

It should come as no surprise at this point that my favorite room in the house is the mudroom. I'd venture to guess most home organizers feel similarly. It fulfills all our purposefully aligned fantasies in much the same way a chef would feel about a well-appointed kitchen. They have their toys and we have ours.

What excites me most about this space is that it can act as a proving ground; if your family can learn to create habits that maintain structure in the mudroom, then it stands to reason that they can do it in the rest of the house too. No excuses. It's all about the systems in place which make learning the routines easier and make the leap to habits seamless. But how does one create those systems when you have nothing in place? The answer comes down to this: know your people. Or in other words, let me pose this question. What is the shortest distance from a coat dropped on the floor to a coat hung on a hook? The answer is, whatever is easiest for the people in your house.

* * *

Allow me to introduce you to Tina's family. She had asked me for some guidance with her and her husband's growing family. They had four children, two biological and two foster children whom they later adopted. Add to the mix Tina's mother who recently moved in with them, and it was a full house to say the least. They were discussing either moving to some place larger or expanding on their current floor plan, but until then they needed immediate help. Right at the front door.

The house did not have a mudroom though there was an area in the family room that could have served the purpose, seeing as it was off the garage. But since the garage had been converted to an in-law suite for her mother, it was no longer used for cars, and therefore, it was no longer an entrance into the house. The only other space was the small front foyer with a coat closet. The space sat at the bottom of the landing to the stairs leading to the second floor and was attached to a center hall that led to the kitchen at the back of the house. We were going to have to use all possible spatial options if there was any hope of order. There wasn't much for Tina and I to discuss when it came to learning the habits of her family. With no system in place, anything would be an improvement over the pile of shoes, coats, and bags that the family was struggling with currently.

I discussed with Tina a modest budget for organizational items; it's true I do prefer to repurpose items from around the house but this project called for a clean slate. There was one glitch, however. Her husband was not on board with having me do any work without his approval of both the plan and the price. I assured her that I have had to convince spouses of the value in my work before and I would be happy to give him a detailed presentation. We scheduled a time for me to come back in the evening the following week.

"That will give me enough time to purchase supplies and put together a written proposal."

"Oh please don't buy anything. My husband doesn't like me spending money," she replied with a touch more uneasiness than I would have liked.

"No worries. He's not spending any money. I'll purchase the items upfront. I don't mark up any of the materials. I will show him all the receipts. And I can return anything that he doesn't think is necessary. You'll only ever pay for the items you keep." I tried to give her a calming smile but she was clearly nervous about this process. Sadly, this was not my first experience with this marital dynamic. I continued, "Let's do it this way. I'll present him a plan where I do the work and another where you and he can do it yourselves. That way, he'll see exactly what my time costs so he can make an educated decision. Now, I'm going to give you some homework. It doesn't need to be done before I meet your husband, but it will need to be done before I start any work. Are you good with that?" I handed her the list entitled "**Homework to Tackle**" and made my exit, all the while hoping Tina's husband was just frugal and not stern.

- **Empty the contents of the hall closet and separate items into piles by the individual owner.**

- **Separate the massive pile of items that is your current mudroom system into the individual owner piles you just made.**

- **Remove from this area anything that is not shoes, backpacks, and outerwear such as coats, hats, gloves, etc. Items to remove may include sports equipment, musical instruments, mail, etc. Ideally, we would**

- **incorporate these items into this area but with limited space to support seven people, it is just not feasible.**

- **Each family member must then decide which items will remain in this space. Each person will be allotted space for two coats, a limited assortment of outerwear accessories, three pairs of footwear, and one handbag or backpack. Beyond that, all items must be moved to their respective bedrooms. Leave the individual piles for me to handle when I come back.**

- **Deep clean the area including inside the hall closet.**

- **Sports equipment remains in the car (a system for weekly clean-outs of both the bags and the car to be implemented).**

* * *

This project was going to be a challenge. A family of seven, an estimated square footage of just 30', and a patriarch who was tight with money and low on compromise. But I like a challenge, so when I went back the following week to meet Tina's husband Fritz, I was ready with three possible proposals and the receipts for the items I purchased for the project.

After a brief conversation on the merits of a household of people each responsible for keeping their possessions neat so the task does not fall to him and Tina alone, I'm happy to report that Fritz was more cheap and cheerful, than miserly and malicious. He chose proposal three.

- Proposal #1 was to hand them the how-to notes to do the work themselves. Cost = supplies plus my time to create the plan.
- Proposal #2 was for me to handle the entire project myself.
- Cost = supplies plus my time and labor plus a handyman for installation.
- Proposal #3 eliminated the handyman if the three of us did the installation work together. Typically I only offer the first two options but I felt with their situation the last one would be the most comfortable for them.
- Cost = supplies plus my time and labor.

NOTE: Some money-conscious clients think that #1 is the way to go, until they realize they have paid me for my plans but the project is still not done. I've had more than a few people choose Option 1 but ultimately call me back to do the work. I, of course, reduce my fee accordingly to reflect what they have already paid. There is value in following through and getting it done versus saving a bit of money and still being left in disarray.

I explained the remainder of the proposal, showed them the items I had purchased, took measurements, and reminded them of the homework list. We scheduled work to be done in two weeks when Fritz could take a day off from work.

* * *

There were a lot of moving parts to this project, but with Tina and Fritz on board, my focus turned to user-friendly and budget-conscious installations, and habit-building procedures. I explained earlier that each of the seven family members would be allotted space for two coats, three pairs of shoes, a backpack or handbag, and a small assortment of seasonal accessories. **My plan was straightforward:**

- **Each child would have their own section of wall space.** Within each space would be two three-prong heavy duty, wrought iron hooks placed one above the other at 2.5' and 5' above the floor. The hooks would be installed on two 2"x4" slats of wood, attached to the wall studs to provide maximum weight allowance. The upper hook would be for coats and a hanging drawstring bag for seasonal outerwear accessories. The lower hook would be for backpacks. Fritz had told me that repainting this space was on his summer to-do list, so we chose to leave the boards natural until then. Easy peasy.

- **Each adult would have a third of the coat closet separated by some sort of divider.** The dividers in this case would be ribbon wrapped around the hanging bar. Wooden hangers only. A bin above each individual's section of the bar. Bins with pull handles on front for easy access off the shelf would be filled with seasonal accessories.

- **Two 24-pocket (or the equivalent of 12 pairs of shoes) hanging shoe bags would be put in place, one behind the front door, the second on the inside of the coat closet.**

NOTE: I cut out a hole, and added a grommet for a finished look, in the center of the hanging bag so the peep hole in the front door could still be accessed.

- **The hanging shoe bag behind the front door would be for the four children, each of which was allotted three pairs of shoes.** Oldest child at the top and working down. Labeling optional.

- **The hanging shoe bag inside the coat closet door was for the three adults, the tallest of**

which would use the top. I chose to leave the pockets closest to eye level free of shoes and suggested those pockets be used for keys, office IDs, sunglasses, etc. since there wasn't room in this area for a console table to hold these errant items.

- **Three additional three-prong hooks would be installed along a wall for the adults' bags.** Also installed on 2"x4" planks of wood attached to the studs, and installed at 2.5' above the floor.

- While these systems provided for clear floor space, **I did suggest two plastic boot trays for foul weather/work boots or for footwear with caked-on dirt** from sports, for example.

- **An indoor/outdoor rug would be laid in the foyer** on the hardwood to minimize dirt being tracked into the house as well as protect the floor beneath from water and elements.

- Lastly, I had done a bit of around-the-house snooping (with Tina's approval) and found **a framed bulletin board I wanted to use for a family master calendar system.** I asked her for some family photos and if she would mind if I took these items home to tinker with it. She agreed. I also planned to hang **a framed**

full-length mirror in the space for those last-minute appearance checks. *It just so happened that I had one unused from a previous project that I gifted to them.*

I made a trip to my local hardware store where they were kind enough to cut all the planks to size based on the measurements I took. I had already purchased the hooks, wooden hangers, bins, shoe bag caddies, and medium drawstring bags. I just had to upcycle Tina's bulletin board into something a bit more decorative. I didn't want the first thing anyone saw as they entered the house to be a jumble of paperwork posing as wall art, but instead a positive expression of the vibrant family that lived here.

NOTE: Creating a decorative bulletin board is a quick and easy way to upgrade not only a boring cork-colored square, but the space it is in. Being organized never has to be dull. Feel free to use one that you found second hand especially since you are going to be covering it with fabric. No one will notice any damage or defects on the cork underneath. If the board you are working with has a standard wood frame, feel free to paint it, or I prefer to wrap the entire piece in fabric and secure to the back with staples *(another use for my electric staple gun)*.

* * *

Let's recap for those of you following along at home. If you are low on space but high on need to organize, then look up at your walls. It doesn't take much to create a well-appointed area and create built-in habits to keep your family's revolving door of activities tidy.

1. **Determine your needs. Then prioritize those needs based on the available space.** You can't put 12 hooks on a foot-long plank of wood. Why? Well, most sturdy hooks are more than an inch wide each AND even if you could, that doesn't leave room to hang coats side by side. Keys maybe, not coats. Think ahead. You may have to consider a wall that is wider than 12" for a family of outerwear.

2. **Don't risk putting hooks into drywall even with wall anchors.** They will not support much weight and certainly not for very long. Hooks on wood planks installed into the wall studs is a permanent solution.

3. **Measure twice. Cut once.** If you are not sure, ask for help from someone who has done this before. Especially when it comes to miter joints where two walls meet. Many hardware stores will cut to specific lengths so you don't have to, but you will not be able to return them if you measure incorrectly.

4. **Don't skimp on product quality even if you are being thrifty.** This is a heavy-duty, high workload space. If you cut corners for a few dollars savings, you may be burdening yourself with future repairs. Done correctly, this space will take a beating and do it for years to come.

5. **Separate so each family member has their own space.** Two important reasons come to mind. One, not searching through everyone else's things to find your own. And two, everyone, even the youngest of the bunch, has their own space to take care of. And just like the opening credits of "Mister Rogers' Neighborhood," the routine of taking off your coat and hanging it followed by taking off your shoes and putting them away becomes a habit-building game. *It's no wonder I used to love Mister Rogers. He spoke to my life-at-right-angles heart before I knew I had one.*

6. **Create systems that allow for floor space.** Get as much as you can off the floor and hung on a bar, in a closet, on a wall hook. Visually, this solves a multitude of organizing issues at a glance. Plus, it's easier to keep neat because people respond best to items at eye level thus putting the idea of neatness front and center.

7. **Cover floors with easy-to-clean, non-skid surfaces.** Coming in with mud on your boots may be easy to clean off of hard surfaces but also slippery. Washable rugs are an ideal compromise.

8. **Don't let the practicality of the space stop you from dressing it up.** Bulletin boards with family calendars and photos make for purposeful wall art. Likewise, letting the kids get creative with their assigned spaces only feeds into their want to keep it neat.

* * *

Organizing comes down to one thing: the ease with which a space can be maintained. If the space cannot be maintained, it's not organized, it's staged. So how do you build in that ease of maintenance to ensure it stays organized? Two things achieve this: less stuff and habit-forming systems in place. That's why I limited the amount each family member could store in this area, ultimately resulting in just those things they use on a regular basis anyway. As for forming habits, having a place to call your own to put your things in a caring and respectful way is the nexus for organizational habits. The kids certainly were not going to learn it from searching a pile for a missing sneaker each morning.

On the day I went back to Tina's, Fritz was not able to

be there after all but he had hung the 2"x4"s and that was the most important part of the project. The rest, I was able to handle myself since Tina had a sick little one home that day. I installed the hooks *(a cordless electric drill is your friend),* hung the shoe caddies, and filled the space with all the items left in piles for me. I labeled the shoe caddy pockets with the children's names so there was no confusion and filled the drawstring bags with their things. I labeled those too. I laid the rug and checked that the front door cleared it easily when opened. Inside the closet, I hung the shoe caddy, filled the bins, placed them on the shelf, and hung the coats on new wood hangers. I hung the full-length mirror on the closet door and secured it with Velcro sticker tabs on the bottom for extra security when the door was in motion.

CLEANING & MAINTENANCE

- With habits in place, this area shouldn't require more than a **weekly vacuuming/washing.** *I love a steam vac for this reason.*
- I would suggest a **serious deep clean of this area at least twice a year.** Think of this seasonally when you are swapping out heavy coats for lighter jackets or muddy boots for flip-flops.
- **Wash or dry clean all items before storing for the season.** Don't forget to empty coat pockets.
- As things that don't belong start working their way back in, **reassess your needs.** There

are extra hooks per person to grow on for this reason.

DECOR JUST FOR TINA

The last task I completed was to hang the new fabric-covered bulletin board. I was so happy with the way the bulletin board turned out, *and I was having so much fun making it the night before that I couldn't stop myself from making matching fabric-covered buttons that I turned into tacks to attach the family photos with.* I positioned the photos around the border so there would be enough space to attach a family chore chart in the center. I had mocked up one of those to get Tina started.

The space was complete. I stepped outside the front door and walked back in to look at it with fresh eyes. It was efficient, user-friendly, and self-explanatory, on top of being very pretty considering it was such a hardworking space. I called out to Tina that I was finished and invited her to take a look before I wrapped up. She came down the stairs with her 7-year-old daughter in tow who was dressed in jammies and a bathrobe. She wanted to see it too.

"Oh, sweetie! What do you think? Do you like it?" Tina said to her daughter in a sing-song voice. Her daughter shook her head "yes" but didn't say a word. She didn't have to. Her eyes lit up when she saw her coat and backpack on their own hooks and her name on the pockets for her shoes. As for Tina, she just looked at me, smiled, and shook her head in disbelief. Then she gave me a side hug saying, "Fritz is going to love it. I might even be able to convince him of more projects."

"I'm ready when you are."

4

Don't Go in There, My Room's a Mess

I love to sleep! Now that I work from home, I nap almost daily. And these aren't 10-minute cat naps on the couch; these are solid REM cycles in bed for at least an hour—*sometimes more if I'm under a weighted blanket.* Just so you don't think I'm a complete sloth, I make up for it by working early mornings and late nights and weekends. In actual fact, it's 1:37am on a Monday morning right now!

But I'm not working from my bed even though it's the literal middle of the night. I would never desecrate my sleeping sanctuary in such a way. Which is the same reason there is no TV, exercise equipment, or baskets of laundry to be folded in my bedroom. None of those things say "ahhh" to me. I believe a bedroom should be an environment for sleeping. Peaceful, restorative, serene sleep. A place where your head hits the pillow, every muscle melts into the mattress, and your breathing instantly becomes deep and rhythmic—*just writing that is making me tired.*

"I want that," you say? Well then let's get to work.

PRACTICALITY. What makes up the best bones of a bedroom?

- Clean, luxurious—*do not assume that means expensive*—bedding.
- Supportive mattress.
- Soft carpeting or rugs.
- Furniture that provides ample storage but not at the expense of floor space.
- Accent lighting.
- Decor that speaks to your personal sense of comfort and tranquility.

Consider this. Hotels employ teams of people who have distilled research down to the above list of very basic essentials for a peaceful night's sleep. Nothing extra, just the very best of what you need. Think about the last hotel room you were in and go through the above checklist. In fact, think about the accent lighting alone; no matter where you sit or stand or lay, you've got a lamp. The reason for that is part practicality, part ambiance. This isn't a kitchen where you need it to be bright in order to work. It's a bedroom where you need to sleep. A place where one person can be reading in a comfy chair under a reading lamp while the other is sleeping in the bed undisturbed.

EFFICIENCY. Let's talk about linens as just one example of where efficiency is to be considered. Ask yourself some questions.

- How many of everything do you own—fitted sheets, flat sheets, pillowcases, throw pillows, blankets, comforters? If your linen storage is overflowing, how much do you actually need? The answer is as much as you actually USE.
- Do you have sheet sets? Do you use sheet sets? Do you mix and match? *I will always be pro-mix and match versus matchy matchy.*
- Are all your linens in good condition? Do you wish some of them were softer, warmer, etc. than they actually are? *Which of course is a leading question because what I'm actually saying is get rid of anything you don't absolutely love.*
- How often do you strip the bed and change linens?
- And all the same questions for bedcovers, blankets, comforters, throws, quilts, coverlets; and yes, as crazy as it sounds, those are all different things.

Whew, and we haven't even discussed the rest

of the room, but let's stick with this theme and do a little math. Even if you change your sheets once a week and choose to put different sheets on your bed each time—*there are times I wait for the clean sheets to come straight out of the hot dryer*—you'd only ever need two sets of sheets. Need being the operative word. But I'm not here to shame you into downsizing your linen collection to just what's currently on your bed. I'm just expanding on my point about excess. **The more you have, the more there is to keep neat and organized. If your goal is organization, less is best.**

ROUTINE. Advice for maintaining your space.

- I'm just gonna say it! MAKE YOUR BED! EVERY DAY! At the very least, pull your covers up so your bedsheets are not exposed.

- Due to the amount of fabric in a bedroom from linens, clothes, window treatments, and the amount of time you spend in your bedroom sleeping, dust from lint, your body, and possibly pet dander, is an absolute given. And it's everywhere! Get on a regular weekly schedule for dusting and vacuuming. That includes vacuuming upholstery. You can do it on the same day you strip the bed and wash sheets.

And while you're at it, put on your calendar monthly or at least quarterly to pull the bed away and vacuum and dust behind it. *That's where the dust bunny warren is.*

- When it comes to clothes, always put them away. That includes your laundry basket filled with clothes from the dryer still to fold. If you can't get to it, leave it in the laundry area. It doesn't belong in the bedroom. And if you are using your laundry baskets as clothing storage, it's time to get rid of some excess clothes.

NOTE: A summary of Chapter 1 from my first book *STOP BUYING BINS* is included at the end of the book for this very reason. We all have more clothes than we wear. We can always benefit from a clear-out.

The idea behind this is simple. If you believe as I do that a bedroom is for rest, recuperation, relaxation and as a byproduct, rejuvenation, then it must exude these traits. There should be no reminders of chores or work to be done, no piles of catchall clutter, only a peaceful oasis to rest your weary bones at the end of a hard-lived day. You must be able to breathe freely in your space, no dust, no noise, no chaos. A jumble-filled bedroom affects your mood in surprisingly negative ways.

DECOR. How to make it your own and what to consider.

- Furniture: Whether you own a matching bedroom suite (a suite usually consists of a headboard sometimes with side rails and a footboard, a dresser sometimes with attached mirror, a chest of drawers, and one or more bedside tables) or you've pulled pieces together for a more organic look, there are three things to consider from a functionality standpoint. Is the furniture to scale for the room? Is the mattress (not included with a suite) comfortable for your tastes and needs? And does the dresser and/or chest of drawers provide you with sufficient storage space? Decor is not just for appearances; practicality for spatial relations and organizing must be considered as well.

- Storage: Speaking of which, ample storage means every piece of clothing has a home. *Which in turn means nothing is ever out of its home unless it is in the laundry or on your body.*

- Decor: Framed photos, jewelry boxes, stack of books, artwork, whatever it is you have on display in your bedroom, keep it to an edited amount, keep it dusted, and keep it on theme with your individual peace of mind in mind.

Regardless of what article you read, the percentage of adults worldwide getting a lousy night's sleep is disturbing—literally. Certainly health problems play a major factor, as do workplace, relationship, and financial stress. But you might also consider that your bedroom and how you keep it bears part of the blame.

The body needs restorative sleep in order to function properly. If you give your bedroom the multiple responsibilities for entertainment, exercise, and a hiding place for clutter, you are in jeopardy of destroying a space meant to soothe and relax you. Your bedroom provides a level of mental restoration that should not be compromised—**therefore, when considering how to organize and decorate, focus on what provides you the best chance at overall well-being, create that version of bliss, and then get rid of the rest.**

* * *

That's what I did for Mikala, who had called me with the colossal project of giving her entire home a furniture placement and organizing facelift. She and her husband were empty nesters, but their adult daughter was moving back in with their newborn grandson. Since both Mikala and her husband had full-time careers where they traveled quite a bit, they had let the house become cluttered and chaotic over the years and that needed to change quickly. She was already familiar with my work since I had done a living room decorating project for her cousin and she therefore trusted me "to give her the same exceptional attention to detail." *Her words.* She explained that she works best with contractors who understand her overall vision but can "take the ball and run with it" as she wasn't interested in "how the sausage is made." As far as she was concerned, I would have complete creative and practical license to do what I saw fit to get the house organized, efficient, and family-friendly. And I had three weeks to do it while she was away on business.

I'm not going to lie; I was thrilled and terrified. Free reign to do whatever I want but still live up to the unexpressed expectations of my client? That's a tall order. One that I happily agreed to, as long as some work was done before I began. We sat down to **create a to-do list** of what I needed her to do before my first day:

- **Go through the entire house collecting trash and recycling as well as putting back any items that needed to find their way to their rightful place.**

- **Do a sweep of the house to collect any items she was immediately aware of that she wanted to donate in order to downsize her belongings.**

- **Secure all valuables like money, jewelry, private papers *(and personal items like the adult toys I came across in another client's home)*.**

- **Do all the laundry as well as wash the sheets and towels currently in use before she left.**

- **Fill and run the dishwasher.**

- **Make a list of all projects she absolutely wanted accomplished.**

- **Alert me to any problems in or with the house.**

- **Alert her neighbors that I would be coming and going for the next few weeks.**

On that first day of work, I met Mikala at 6am ahead of her flight to Chicago for her three-week business trip. She handed me my own set of keys as soon as I entered the house, gave me a quick tutorial for using the alarm system, and walked me through the house to show me she had indeed done the homework I assigned. Coincidentally, her husband was away in Prague for work for at least another month so I would have complete access to her home. *For those of you who know me, you know I was buzzing to get started. Three weeks to work uninterrupted with no explanations and complete control? Jackpot! I hope it didn't show on my face how eager I was for her Uber to show up so I could be alone with the adrenaline coursing through my veins.*

Given the size of this project, I could quite easily have used it as the example for every chapter of this book. But I chose to use Mikala's bedroom to emphasize my original point of creating bliss and relaxation. Long story short, the first time I saw the primary bedroom, I thought it was an oversized—and not-well-organized—walk-in closet because in all honesty, that's what it looked like.

The main bedroom in this 1960's ranch was, to put it bluntly, small and the windows and doors were in odd locations in the room. On top of which, Mikala and her husband had an ornate, weighty suite of furniture. Added to the collection was a dressing table and chair which were being used as a catchall. She had warned me that whenever they had company, she would just throw whatever clutter was around the house into her bedroom to hide it. Every bit of usable space was taken up by furniture, laundry baskets, suitcases, and shopping bags. The walking area in the room was reduced to a pathway that snaked around the piles. It was by far the worst room in the house…and therefore, my starting point.

I've said many, many times to "start small" when it comes to organizing projects but this was an atypical assignment. Because of the scope of the overall project, I decided to take a different route to getting it all done. The only way I was going to get through this room was by chipping away at it a piece at a time. I planned to start each day working in the bedroom, then when I felt like I needed a break or a change of scenery, I would move onto another smaller space or activity somewhere else in the house. By the end of each work day, I would have completed both an area of the house and a bit more of the bedroom. My hope was that in giving myself enough breaks, I wouldn't lose momentum.

* * *

Let's take a **step-by-step look at the process so you too can tackle the work** in your own home. Before you begin, **devise a grand plan with a new look for the room based first and foremost on use and practicality.** Remember that you can have a beautiful room that looks incredible in photos but can't be used OR a room that still looks beautiful but centered around the concept of functionality, giving you the best chance at keeping it neat and organized. Consider the following when planning the layout of furniture:

- **If your furniture is overpowering in the space, consider removing a few pieces or purchasing smaller ones.** "But then I won't have enough storage for all my things." You know what I'm going to say to that. "Looks like you're going to have to get rid of some of your things."

- **When arranging furniture in the room, consider walkways to and from and around each piece.** You should be able to walk a fairly straight line between your most obvious destinations—from the door to the bed, from the bed to the bathroom, from the bathroom to the dresser, on which you should be able to open drawers fully while standing in front of them. There should be enough room around each piece of furniture to maneuver effortlessly without brushing up against and bending around pieces.

- **Keep windows free from visual blocks.** This is a feng shui principle to allow for flow of good energy but it is also for visual harmony to be able to see out of your windows as well as allow sunlight in. As such, window treatments for privacy at night should be drawn back during the day. This also provides safe access to windows in the event of an emergency. *I may have watched too many fire-safety PSAs during Saturday morning cartoons as a kid.*

NOTE: Natural light in a home is vitally important to your family's health and overall sense of well-being. Sunlight boosts mood, adds extra heat during the winter months, gives a visual sense of openness and space thus making your room look bigger, connects you to the natural world outside, and can even improve the air quality inside the home. So let the sunshine in!

- **Doors, drawers, wardrobe doors should all be able to open fully and freely.** This is not only necessary for use but to avoid the unconscious sense of being confined or trapped within your space anywhere in the house. *Not being able to open your bedroom door fully because there is something behind the door you keep knocking into is blocking your energy.*

- **Do not feel obligated to continue to hold onto anything you don't use.** This applies to anything from flat top sheets *(there has been a surprising debate on this issue in the last decade)* to dressing tables, which have gone out of fashion as most people apply their makeup in the bathroom.

- **Anything in your bedroom that is counter to rest and rejuvenation should be removed and housed elsewhere.** *YOUR BEDROOM IS NOT A STORAGE UNIT!*

Now that you have a working plan for furniture placement in your room based on spatial relations and functionality, it's **time to make it all happen. Let's break down the steps:**

1. **If you are attempting to work through your ENTIRE HOUSE, make a plan for both the largest project as well as a list of small 30-minute long projects.** You don't want to waste any time making decisions about what to do when you can be working.

2. Assuming you are working in the primary bedroom as your main project: **Make the bed, then cover with a sheet. This is your workstation.**

3. **Gather an assortment of empty bins/boxes/laundry baskets to use for sorting. Place them on the bed. Have one bin assigned to things that belong in other rooms of the house and have that bin near the door.**

4. **Now, create a mental 9-box grid of the bedroom; think tic-tac-toe board. Assign the space to the left of the door as area #1. Work around the room clockwise ending in the center. In a primary bedroom, the center space will likely be the bed.**

5. **Pull out everything from area #1. Leave nothing behind. Sort the contents into the bins.** Possible categories: clothes, books, donate.

6. With the space clear, **decide what adjustments you will be making to the furniture, either moving pieces in or out of area #1. If you are moving furniture into that space, empty the furniture first, sort what came out, then place the piece in area #1.**

7. **Do a cursory cleaning of any furniture now placed in area #1.**

8. **Move onto area #2 and repeat all the same steps. Then again in each area.**

9. **Before you move onto area #5 (which is likely the head of the bed), take a break to sort through your boxes. First, take another opportunity to downsize the piles.** *I guarantee you can always find more to get rid of.* **If you know a specific pile will eventually be organized into areas #1-#4, go ahead and place that pile there.** But don't waste time now in making it look pretty. This step is only to give you more working space as you go.

10. **Continue through each area until each has just the furniture you planned for that space and the pile of items that will be organized into that space.**

NOW THE ORGANIZING CAN BEGIN IN EARNEST! THAT'S RIGHT, WE'VE ONLY PREPPED FOR ORGANIZING! Yes, at this point the room looks as bad or worse than it did when you started but remember the old saying, "It's always darkest before the dawn." So before we go any further, let's take a breather and I'll tell you more of Mikala's story.

* * *

Floor plan and to-do list in hand, empty bins at the ready, and grande cappuccino kicking in, I prepared myself for battle in Mikala's primary bedroom. First things first, I made the bed so I would have somewhere to work. I covered the bed with a clean flat sheet I had brought and topped that with four empty bins to use for sorting and shuffling.

Area #1 of the imaginary tic-tac-toe was that useless space behind the bedroom door. In this case though it was being used for a collection of suitcases that prevented the door from fully opening. To add more to the first task of the day, the suitcases were all filled with clothes. *Oh man, the first obstacle of the day and it wasn't even 7am!* I texted Mikala to ask if they were filled with laundry from a previous trip or if she was storing clothes in them. She said she had no idea; she hadn't used them in almost a year since buying sturdier luggage. *<Insert eye roll here.>* No worries, I had planned to leave that area empty all along, so I put the suitcases in the laundry room to deal with later and I moved onto area #2.

Area #2 held the aforementioned dressing table and upholstered stool, and both were piled high with shopping bags. The shopping bags were filled with Christmas gifts Mikala had purchased on her travels. During my previous planning stage, I toyed with the idea of turning her son's old bedroom into a playroom for the baby, so I moved all the shopping bags there, along with some errant rolls of gift wrap I remembered seeing in the hall closet and reclassified her son's old bedroom as the play/crafts/gift-wrapping room. There was always the potential for that idea to change down the road but it was a good one for now.

Once I uncovered the dressing table, it was covered with jewelry, makeup, and old perfume bottles. From their condition, these items hadn't been used in months, maybe years. I cleared off the table top, emptied the drawers, separated the items into bins, then wiped the half inch of dust off the table, mirror, and stool before moving it all into Mikala's daughter's room to use there once it became the nursery/bedroom when they moved in.

I was in a good groove with my pace and energy and not losing any focus to the hiccups so far, but that was all about to change. Mikala had a piece of furniture I wanted to move to area #2 but it was not to be. Taking up nearly a full wall opposite the bed was a vintage three-piece wardrobe. Each piece was somewhere between three to four feet wide and almost reached the ceiling. In my overambitious initial walkthrough of this house, I thought I would be able to shift one of the three wardrobes to replace the dressing table and stool. That idea went right out the window when I discovered these wardrobes were not only brittle and damaged with age making moving them hazardous, but that they were actually bolted to the wall with childproofing straps because of their fragility.

Time to come up with a Plan B while emptying those full suitcases into the washing machine and running it, before consolidating each suitcase into the other like a Russian stacking doll and storing them in the basement. *Thank God, the basement was not part of this three-week project. I didn't have the stamina for that.*

NOTE: Home organizing is not done until it's done and even once it's done, it needs continued revisions. The best laid plans in your head or even on paper with precise measurements can turn out being just-not-right once you put it together. You have to remain flexible for the eventuality of having to stop everything and problem-solve a situation. This mishap could take the form of:

- finding a missing item you haven't laid eyes on in months (which may cause you to get distracted with a new project)
- pulling a muscle lifting a heavy box (which may cause you to be out of commission)

- breaking or spilling something (which needs to be cleaned immediately)
- running out of a needed supply like hangers (which stops all progress)
- or finding out after you've moved a piece of furniture across the room that it doesn't actually fit where you want to put it—*been there, done that.*

Since I couldn't move the wardrobe to area #2, I decided instead to leave the space empty for the moment instead of wasting time thinking of an alternative. The first two areas in this room had been taken up with items that didn't belong there in the first place. **Now, there was room for space—a concept far too often overlooked. Every corner of your home doesn't need to be filled.**

Area #3 was next and let's just say I considered making this a chapter all its own. *Let's call this Chapter 4½.* When you are working in your own home, you may feel more comfortable skipping this and coming back after you have completed the rest of the bedroom but here goes nothing—onto the walk-in closet! For Mikala, it was really more of a slide-in-sideways closet. This is going to take a bit of explaining and even after you read this through, you will have to customize my advice for your own space. But don't fret! I promise this will be fun! *Maybe that's just me and my weird sense of "fun" but at least you'll get a clean closet out of it.* Let's start with some clothes hanger basics.

Stop Pushing Perfection

* * *

"No wire hangers!" Mommy Dearest reference aside, I don't like them either. Nor do your clothes. But like so many things in the home organizing world, hangers are not a one-size-fits-all proposition so I'm just going to give you the pros and cons so you can decide for yourself. One thing I will hold firm to for continuity and the look of a well-organized closet—they must be consistent across all the clothes in a given category.

Wire Hangers (usually from the dry cleaners, though they can be purchased and those are usually plastic coated)

PROS:
Wire hangers are thin, making it easy to fit more of them, and therefore more clothes, in your closet.

CONS:
Wire hangers are unattractive, they bend easily with use or weight of clothes, they leave folds/puckers in clothes at the edges, and they were never meant to be the standard for home use.

Felt/Velvet-Covered Hangers (readily available in multiple colors to match your decor, though my advice is to stick to neutrals like all black or ivory)

PROS:
Velvet-covered hangers are only slightly thicker than wire hangers so you can still fit more into your closet, fabric prevents clothes from slipping off and as such clothes can be positioned on hangers at the seams for less visible puckers.

CONS:
With velvet-covered hangers, removing clothes from the hangers can be frustrating because the fabric's purpose is to prevent them from slipping, and as a result, they are quick to break when pulled.

PRO BONUS: With velvet-covered hangers you won't need those hateful loops in your blouses and dresses that are meant to hold them on hangers. Cut them out! *All they ever wind up doing is sneaking out of the neckline and arm holes while you're wearing them.*

Plastic (readily available in multiple colors to match your decor, though my advice is to stick to neutrals like all white)

PROS:
Plastic hangers are readily available in multiple colors.

CONS:
Plastic hangers take up more room on the bar, come in different quality levels so some will break more easily, leave folds and puckers on clothes at the edges, and will bend if used for pants.

Padded (available in multiple colors and patterns to match your decor, usually made of satin)

PROS:
Padded hangers do not leave any puckers on clothes, are ideal for structured items with shoulder pads, and are pretty and feminine.

CONS:
Padded hangers limit greatly the amount of items you can hang on a bar because they are bulky, cannot be used for anything but blouses/blazers, straight shoulder angle prevents use with all shirts, and they are pricier than even wood hangers.

Wood (available in natural wood but also painted to match your decor)

PROS:
Wood hangers are the gold standard for a beautiful designer closet, they are sturdy for a wide range of fabric weights, some have rubber grips at the shoulder to prevent slipping, and they virtually never break.

CONS:
Wood hangers do limit the amount of items you can hang on a bar due to their size, be aware that some do not come with a cross bar for hanging pants though you can also purchase wood hangers with clips for pants or skirts.

My personal preference is velvet-covered hangers in black for all tops and dresses, and wood hangers in natural for jackets/blazers, sweaters (folded; I'll explain later), and pants. I find that with these I get the best of all pros with very little cons.

NOTE: Save yourself some cash and don't purchase hanging closet organizers with the idea that they will get you organized. They take up room, provide insufficient space anyway, and annoyingly swing when you try to put things in them. They are frustrating and useless. There are better ways to organize. But on a separate note, do purchase inexpensive garment bags to cover clothes you are not wearing (seasonal or eventwear) to protect them from dust. Okay. Ready? Roll up your sleeves, we're going in!

1. **Pull everything out of the closet.** Nothing stays behind that isn't attached. **Then clean the closet—dust, vacuum, wash the walls and floor if you have to.** We're starting with a clean slate.

2. ASSUMING YOU HAVE ALREADY DOWNSIZED YOUR CLOTHES TO JUST WHAT FITS AND JUST WHAT YOU ARE WEARING ON A REGULAR BASIS (read "It Bears Repeating", near the end of this book, for an excerpt from *STOP BUYING BINS*), you should now **separate your clothes into piles based on clothing type: shirts, pants, skirts, dresses, sweaters, etc.**

3. Time for a game! **Remove 2-10 additional pieces from each pile and put them in a bag to donate.** Game over! You won!

4. **Take one of the clothing piles and sort further** (to make these instructions easier, I am going to use shirts/tops as my example). Sort shirts into categories. Possible examples: dressy, casual, sleeveless, short-sleeved, long-sleeved, heavyweight like flannel, lightweight like seersucker. In my own closet, I do them all. *I know, I know. It's just how I'm wired.*

5. **Replace all the hangers with one consistent style and color. If you are right-handed, the hanger head (that's the curved part that hooks on the bar) should be open to the left like a question mark and the front of the shirt facing you when you hold it in your dominant hand.** Same if you are left-handed, only the opposite. This is for ease of motion. Your dominant hand pushes or pulls the hangers across the bar and in this way you will always see the front of the shirt. *However, many left-handed people have learned to live in a right-handed world thus making my last three sentences null and void. You do you!*

6. **Immediately bag the hangers you are no longer using. Donate or give away.** *Check ahead. The last time I was at Goodwill they had a sign posted saying "No Hanger Donations." Just find a way to get them out of your house. You don't need them.*

7. **Starting with just the sleeveless shirts, put them all on the bar. Now rearrange them in color order.** "What the heck, Bonnie? Seriously?" By all means, if you want to stop at just separating your clothes by shirt, pants, etc., then have at it. If your current closet has your clothes all mixed together in a great big fabric soup, then separating out your shirts to keep together in one place is already an improvement. But if you are looking to go a bit, or a lotta bit, further…start with white, work through tonal beige neutrals from light to dark, followed by greys and black, then proceed with the colors in rainbow order: red, orange, yellow, green, blue, purple. **Move onto the short-sleeved shirts and do the same. And so on through the rest of the shirts, then onto dresses, pants, etc.**

Let me make this easier on you by giving you some theory. The point of all this minutiae is:

- **to make your closet look orderly**
- **to make getting dressed easier**
- **to have an easier system in order to keep it organized**

Those three points are the basis for all closet organizing but even they have to be put through your personal filters based on your personal situation.

For the purpose of example, let's say you live in Florida year round and spend all your time in Lilly Pulitzer sportswear. You may want to prioritize your pieces by pattern for ease in matching. Maybe you work in retail and have a standard uniform of red tops and khaki bottoms (á la Target). Your best path is probably to have all your red tops next to all your khaki bottoms placed front and center in your closet. Or if you're like me, you will want your clothes sorted out first by product, then maintenance level, then style, then color. *Of course, life is so much easier now that I work from home as a writer and wear loungewear 90% of the time.*

Boutique retail stores on the other hand create their floor plans around one color, then style, then size. But your closet is not something out of a sci-fi movie where you own multiples of one grey jumpsuit with insignia patch. *At least I don't think so.* Having all the white shirts in your closet together in length order would look just like a boutique, but practically speaking, you are less likely to dress by color and more likely to dress for the weather. With that in mind, having all your white shirts together solely because it looks good that way on the bar doesn't make as much sense as all your sleeveless shirts together en masse so that when it's going to be hot as hell, you can go directly to that section instead of looking in white, then in green, then in purple. "Oh good God, Bonnie! This is too much!" I know it seems that way. But only at first and then I promise, it becomes muscle memory.

NOTE: I no longer have to get dressed in career clothes, *since my office is in my living room and I'm the only one who works here.* Any dressier blouses that I still have hang to the far left in my closet. They too follow the sleeve length then color rule, but I don't need to see them every day so no need to work them into the space front and center when I open the french doors to my closet. That leaves most of the bar for all my day-to-day clothes.

We're almost done so let's keep going.

8. **Hangers for dresses—velvet-covered with the exception of dresses with beading.** I learned this tidbit in my early 20s. I was at a wedding, and the mother of a friend of mine was wearing a beaded dress which over the course of the evening got longer. The beads were weighing it down and stretching the silk.

These dresses are best folded with clean archival tissue paper and boxed. But for the rest of your dresses, use the sorting system already discussed.

9. **Hangers for pants—wood.** Word of warning: **Be aware of dust.** If you are not wearing them regularly, be aware that dust will settle on the fold of the leg and eventually fade the fabric. Dust off, rotate, put them in garment bags, or wear and clean regularly. Whatever you do, don't let them sit. **This goes for blazers, suits, coats which should also be on wood hangers, which are both sturdier for the added weight of these pieces and for keeping the structure of the jacket.**

10. **Hangers for sweaters—wood, not hung like a shirt, but hung like pants.** I mentioned earlier I would get to the rationale behind hanging sweaters. **Yes, folding and stacking sweaters is the best option for the sweater.** BUT, try pulling out one from the middle of a stacked pile from a shelf above your head and they all come tumbling down. Not an ideal scenario for you or for maintaining your closet. In a perfect world we would all have wardrobes like a C.S. Lewis novel, with room for a Narnia's worth of woolens, folded and stacked at eye level. But

since most of us do not, *and if you are a shorty like myself,* this hanging trick keeps sweaters neat and easily accessible. **Fold in half down the center, fold the now lined up sleeves, in and down, fold over a wooden hanger bar like pants. Again, you will have to be wary of dust build-up on the fold.**

Whew! Are you as exhausted as I am? Holy moly! I need a nap! Let's get out of the closet and get back to the bedroom. Things should go faster from here.

We are now in area #4 in Mikala's room; her bed and two bedside tables occupy this space. I was currently using the bed as my staging area so I would be leaving that for last. As for the bedside tables, I have a love/hate relationship with them in general. Going back in time they have been used as everything from a place to set a candle lantern in the event that villagers came knocking and you had to see your way to the door, a revolver if you were on the run from the sheriff, or a clock radio set to your favorite station to wake you for school with the dulcet tones of a morning DJ. Unfortunately, in my experience, they are more of a catchall for junk, *and to put it bluntly, I don't want garbage to be the first thing I see in the morning, nor do I want it piled next to my head.*

I don't own bedside tables. Yes, that means that I usually fall asleep with a book, a water bottle, and my phone in the bed with me, but I see that as a small price to pay for not having to dust another piece of furniture. I may be a party of one on this subject so for anyone with bedside tables, let's clean them up, shall we?

- Necessities only. That's maybe a lamp, a clock, a phone charger (but avoid cords in the bed; there are many articles on why), a jewelry dish (for your everyday items only, e.g., watch, wedding bands if you remove them at night), a coaster for your drinking glass or mug (notice I said coaster only; you're not storing used dishes), a few books (that are currently in reading rotation), possibly a pad and pen for middle-of-the-night thoughts and reminders.

- If you have a drawer, well, frankly, I don't want to give a reason for this space because I've never seen a bedside drawer used for anything but junk.

- Avoid almost anything else. My least favorite items on a bedside table are pill bottles (for anyone other than the bedridden, that is). You are waking up to a new day. Please don't remind yourself of ailments first thing in the morning.

Now the same system applies.

1. **Strip the area of everything but furniture.**

2. **Sort items into bins or piles.**

3. **Pull furniture away from the wall and clean all sides inside and out.**

4. **Deep vacuum behind the bed and the back of the headboard. Vacuum any electrical cords and the outlets themselves.** Between the dust-causing elements near this wall all the time and any electrical outlets creating a magnetic charge, dust and hair accumulates in great heaping amounts behind the bed.

5. **Slide furniture back into place.**

6. **Because this is (or should be) a low-maintenance space, go ahead and put the items you need here, back neatly.**

Easy peasy! Onto area #5. Stacks of laundry baskets filled with assorted items lined the space in the corner of the room. There was also a chair, but not a plush reading chair, just a wooden dining chair that was clearly put there to lay stuff on. Not wanting to lose my steam, I put the laundry baskets on the bed and the chair in the kitchen, then swept out the space and moved onto area #6. I would deal with the contents in time.

If you are following along on your tic-tac-toe board, area #6 is the center space on the right-hand wall. In Mikala's room there was a large window that looked out into the side yard with a big beautiful oak tree providing plenty of privacy. But even still, there were several layers of draperies on the window: roller shades, sheer panels, heavy tapestry side panels, and a swag valance. They were far too heavy for this small and overcrowded space, collecting dust and cobwebs, and not truly providing security. This was the moment when I told myself "she did give you free reign to do whatever," and I took it.

First thing to go was the valance, so caked with dust and cobwebs that I pulled my shirt up over my mouth and nose. I slid it off the rod directly into a garbage bag to deal with later. I was sure that Mikala had spent thousands of dollars on these window treatments so I would give her the final say of what to do with them once she got home. The window and the room as a whole already looked lighter and airier. Next to go were the sheer panels. Gone! They serve no purpose. I understand they were at one point the standard for window treatments and for some reason many people have bought into the idea that they are a must. They are no more a must in today's world than petticoats are, and at least petticoats served a purpose. For the moment, I left the side panels and the roller shades for final adjustments at the end of the whole project.

Now, remember that three-piece vintage wardrobe

attached to the wall so it wouldn't fall and crush someone while they slept? Meet area #7 and #8. *I actually said a little prayer before opening them up to see what was inside, and once I did, I took my lunch break. It was THAT overwhelming for me and I do this for a living.*

Speaking of taking a break, **let's take a quick look at what we've done so far.**

1. **We decided how best to lay out the furniture and consider removing oversized or mismanaged pieces if they serve no purpose.**

2. **We covered the bed to use as a staging area and topped with empty bins for sorting.**

3. **We imagined the room as a nine-box grid like a tic-tac-toe-board and assigned the space to the left of the door as area #1 working in a clockwise manner.**

4. **We removed all the items from the one area, including furniture if it is leaving the space. Any furniture staying was emptied and cleaned. Any furniture being moved to the space was emptied and moved in. The area was given a quick clean. We also considered streamlining pieces of furniture that all too often became dumping grounds.**

5. All the items pulled from the space were sorted into bins.

6. We moved onto the next space and did the same. And considered leaving blank open spaces as a form of decorating.

7. When it comes to the primary closet, we matched hangers to essential elements for the longevity of each piece of clothing and the neatness of the closet.

8. Clothes were sorted, rehung on proper hangers, then hung in the closet as described previously, or some version that best suits the personal style, so long as the end goal was to maintain efficiency first, look second.

9. We reduced layers of window treatments that serve little to no purpose or ultimately blocked sunlight.

10. And we took breaks *(like this one)* whenever necessary to recharge focus and motivation. It is the reason for the 9-box grid. So you always have a starting and stopping point.

We are almost there! Visualize the reward for all your hard work. *I was visualizing a hot bubble bath and Chinese takeout when the day was through.*

I opened all three wardrobes to take in the full scope of their contents. The first one appeared to be her husband's things. I had previously decided to give him his own closet in their son's old room and add it to the multi-use of the play/craft/gift wrap room, so without hesitation, I moved all his things there to deal with another day. As a result, this one move freed up an entire wardrobe to turn into a linen closet or perhaps spillover of other categories. The middle wardrobe was mostly bedding, jewelry, and intimates (e.g., underwear, bras, socks, including pajamas). I pulled it all out and made the appropriate piles, with the exception of the jewelry which I left to sort where it was. This section of the wardrobe had built-in velvet-lined jewelry drawers and stands; it was currently a tangle of gold and silver but I knew I could get it into shape. The last wardrobe had Mikala's sweaters, jeans, activewear, and shoes. I pulled them out too and got to sorting. That was the last of the spaces cleared and cleaned.

The feeling I had at that moment was one I hope you experience too. Yes, it was still a vision of disorganization, but pulling it all out, assessing what is there, pondering the space, and envisioning the beautiful end result, all of that is freeing and inspiring. Knowing that you are on the verge of change, of living a better, easier life just by organizing your things—it's so powerful.

The next step is always my favorite. This is the moment you get to put it all back together. Take your time and enjoy it. This is, for an artist, like putting paint to canvas after you've sketched it out. And my vision for Mikala wasn't just putting it all back in crisper stacks and straighter rows. I wanted to give her a version of peace that only Greece could provide. Again, that little voice in my head said "go ahead, she told you to do whatever you wanted" so wading past the piles on the floor, I ran down to the living room and lifted a large framed painting of a Mykonos coastline off the wall. Not only was Mikala from Mykonos, but the painting was done by her late father. I couldn't imagine a better way to wake up each morning than to see this painting as she rolled out of bed. I hung it where the dressing table had been, thus replacing piles of shopping bags and unused furniture with the Aegean blues and whites of her homeland. I was very pleased with myself, and with a big ol' smile on my face, I went back to the wardrobes.

* * *

Here are some bedroom basics to put the final touches on things.

LINEN CLOSET (newly assigned to wardrobe one in Mikala's room)

- Separate your linens: fitted sheets, flat sheets, standard pillowcases, king pillowcases, etc. "Why separate them and not put them into sets?" You can of course put them in sheet sets, but after a few chapters you know how I feel about matchy matchy anything, preferring to mix and match. *As for why, if you need just one piece and you have them in sets, now you are stuck breaking up a set.*

- Refold all the flat sheets for continuity. No need to explain how to fold a rectangular sheet. You do you. Just make them all the same. Then follow suit with the pillowcases.

- Refold all the fitted sheets. *It would be easier to show you but this is a book and I can't draw.* I'm going to do my best to explain it.
    → fold in half, top to bottom
    → tuck one end into the other, lining up the corner seams
    → let the fabric fold in naturally
    → straighten folds to as close to a sharp rectangle as you can get
    → fold as you would a flat sheet

- Place each stack next to each other on a shelf. *Now you can mix and match to your heart's content.*

- Refold blankets, quilts, bedspreads, etc. to approximately the same size as each other and stack by seasonal use, putting the season you are in at the top of the pile.

JEWELRY (wardrobe two in Mikala's room)

- Separate jewelry into categories: necklaces, bracelets, earrings, etc.

- Spend some time pairing up earrings. Use what jewelry storage options you already have. A pile doesn't count as an option. If you don't have a compartmental jewelry box or a slotted earring holder, mini ziplock or drawstring fabric bags are a great option. Available online or at any craft store.

- Spend some time untangling chain necklaces and bracelets. Tweezers, a safety pin, and a bright light to work by are all you need. If you don't have a compartment jewelry box or the boxes they came in, mini 3"x5" ziplock baggies are a great option.

- Note any watches that need new batteries or professional cleanings and take care of that as soon as possible.

- If you are using the baggie system, find an attractive, low-profile box or container to put them all in. Store in a drawer.

INTIMATES (wardrobe two in Mikala's room)

- Separate underwear/panties *(I hate that word)*, bras, socks, any other items in this category that you have.

- You can do as much or as little as you'd like as long as you keep each category separated from each other or paired together in the case of socks. Speaking of which, I prefer to pair and fold socks than make balls. Balling them overstretches the elastic. *And as far as underwear is concerned, I fold mine in thirds side to side then in thirds top to bottom—just in case you were wondering.*

- If you own negligees and you have the room to hang them, those pretty padded hangers I mentioned earlier are the way to go. Same with silky robes.

- There was more room in wardrobe two so I moved activewear into this space.

- Tops and bottoms separated and folded to somewhat equal size. Then placed in drawers, laying them slightly off from each other like stair steps so you can see them all. If you don't have the space to do that, stacking them works too.

JEANS & SWEATERS (wardrobe three in Mikala's room)

- Separate jeans by wash or color.

- Fold in half lengthwise at the zipper. Pull out the crotch so it makes almost a right angle to the pant leg. Fold in thirds; in most cases that's roughly ankle to just below the crotch and then again.

- Stack on a shelf. If you are working with a drawer, because of the stiffness of denim, you should be able to place them on their end; like seeing them on a shelf, but instead looking down on them in a drawer. That of course only works if the drawer is deep enough. For shallow drawers, stacking them and then laying them slightly off from each other like stair steps, if possible, is your best option.

- Separate sweaters by bulkiness and then color.

- Lay crew neck, turtleneck, half-zip neck (zipped up) sweaters face down. Fold arms in at the sleeve seam straight across shoulders. Fold in sides until they touch down the back of the sweater. Fold in half from bottom. Flip over. Turtlenecks fold down. Stack in color order.

- Button or zip cardigans. Ideally hang on padded hangers the same way you would a shirt. If folded, follow the instructions above for hanging sweaters.

- This is all assuming you have the shelf space for sweaters . If not, refer to the hanging option in the closet section above.

SHOES (also in wardrobe three in Mikala's room)

There are many ways to organize shoes and all of them have pros and cons. From shoe racks on the floor to shoe pockets that hang behind a door, unless you have the infinite space of a celebrity closet, you are kind of making it up as you go along with what you have and within your budget. The problem with shoes is their structure. You can't fold them smaller and squeeze one more in—and if you could, what do you do with the second shoe? So here are my suggestions for how to make it work for you.

- Really pare, *pun intended*, down your shoe collection.

- Store seasonal shoes (snow boots to flip-flops) with your seasonal items (winter coats to beach towels) to reduce your main inventory.

- Divide your shoes between "the regulars" and "the occasionals". Keep the regulars in some organized fashion at or near the door (we talked about this in the last chapter). Keep the occasionals in your closet.

- For the occasionals, separate shoes into categories: sneakers, flats, loafers, heels, etc.

- Line the pairs facing you.

- Line your racks or hanging pockets with the shoes by category most-likely-to to least-likely-to wear. Most-likely-to should be in a position easiest to access.

- Any fabric (satin, etc.) dressy shoes should be boxed to keep dust from destroying them.

- I do NOT believe you need to purchase individual shoe bins to house your shoes in great stacks. And if you have them, I certainly wouldn't go to the trouble of taking a photo of the shoes and attaching it to the outside of the box, as other home organizers suggest. If the boxes are clear, you can see the shoes inside. But while bins appear to make everything neat for storing, they take up a lot of space and, more importantly, make the shoes difficult to access. *Your goal is not to organize your shoes so you can look at them. Your goal is to organize so you can keep it neat once you dare to actually wear a pair.*

- Shoes will get dusty, the insides too. If your shoes have dust bunnies living in them, that's your sign to get rid of them, *both the shoes and the bunnies.* You arc just not wearing them enough for them to take up space.

And with the last pair of shoes on the rack, I only had decorating to get to.

CLEANING & MAINTENANCE

As utterly exhausting as it is to pull it all out and put it back together with organization in mind, the work involved and the **new routines and systems in place** will make it more than worth the effort.

- **Stick to a cleaning calendar.** If you have a housekeeper, they are already on a schedule, but if you are cleaning for yourself, **pick a day**. Mondays always seemed to be my day. I think it has something to do with starting off the week with a clean slate. Speaking of which, here are some habits to get used to:

- **MAKE YOUR BED EVERY DAY!**
- **Put away your clothes, shoes, jewelry immediately after taking them off.** Either back in their homes or in the laundry basket. They don't live on the floor or tossed on a chair.
- **Put away laundry baskets of clothes immediately. Or leave them undone in the laundry area.** It's a mental cue. Once the gallimaufry gets a foothold in your space, it will grow. Don't cultivate it.
- **Strip your bed weekly and remake with fresh sheets or wait for them, warm from the dryer** but remake it soon after or you run the risk of being too tired to make your bed and just sleeping on the mattress pad. It happens for clients more than I realized.
- **On the days you strip the bed, dust and vacuum the room as well.** Feather dusting is fine if you do it regularly or with a furniture cleaner at least quarterly.
- Remember what I said about those dust bunnies at the start of this chapter. **Pull the**

furniture away from walls and vacuum behind them. It gets furry fast.

→ **Windex all mirrors, glass-front artwork. and framed photos at least monthly but every other week is best.** When they sparkle in the sun instead of accentuating the dust and fingerprints, the reason for cleaning them so often will be clear.

- **Do NOT use your bedroom as a hiding place.** I remember years ago, my daughter was at a classmate's house for a playdate. The mother and I were chatting in the kitchen when my daughter called down to me to come upstairs and see the little girl's room. The mother reached out and took my hand saying, "Please don't go upstairs. It's a mess," her eyes pleading. "My life is kinda falling apart and this," she said pointing around the elegant main floor rooms "is all smoke and mirrors." I smiled back and called up to my daughter, "That's okay baby, we'd better get home." It was then and there that I vowed to myself and all future clients that I would never let them treat company better than themselves. Don't squirrel away clutter in your bedroom so that your guests think your home is always company-ready. That's just an upside-down perspective to take. If you want your home always pristine, ready for the neighbor who pops in, then organize your home so it IS always pristine or at least presentable. And for heaven's sake, put all the clutter in the garage or some other classically unkempt space. **Your bedroom should never be a catchall.**

DECOR JUST FOR MIKALA

The next morning when I arrived at Mikala's house, I walked from room to room collecting items I thought would work with the theme I was creating in her bedroom. I found another painting her father had done, not quite as large as the other, but horizontal so ideal above the bed. I had also gathered throw pillows, an area rug, two rimmed oval dishes, and an upholstered armchair I hadn't noticed during my first tour because it was under a bunch of baby clothes she had purchased for her grandson. Everything I had collected was in shades of blue and crisp white. **Shopping from your stash** is one of my favorite decorating tricks. We all have plenty of items that, if reworked into new rooms with new purposes, can bring new life to your space.

First things first, I made the bed with new linens all in white from the newly organized wardrobe. Even that task was easy breezy. I chose a white comforter, a blue throw for the foot of the bed, and three throw pillows in shades of blue, turquoise and white for a bit of color in front of the bed pillows. I replaced the jewelry dish already on Mikala's bedside table with one of the cobalt glass ones I found and put the other on her husband's table. I laid the area rug on her husband's side of the bed since it was one of his only requests and the armchair I set at an angle near the large painting I hung the day before. I pulled the bed away from the wall and hung the second painting with enough clearance above the headboard. Then I left the room, took a deep breath, and reentered to see how it all came together.

Now it was time to ask myself some questions. Did the room feel inviting? Was there anything blocking my path from point A to B both physically and visually? Did the drawers and wardrobe doors open without impact into something else? When I opened drawers and doors, were the contents easy to see and, more importantly, easy to access? Did everything make sense for where it was? Did it seem effortless to "work" in this space? Was the closet easy to navigate, meaning everything was in a space that seemed intuitive? Did this room feel restful but also joyful?

I'm pleased to say I could almost feel the breeze off the Aegean Sea. I couldn't wait for Mikala and her husband to see it, or better yet, wake up in it. It was no longer a space to crash at the end of the day. It was a space to look forward to spending time in.

* * *

I was in Mikala's home every day for those three weeks and there were things I still would have done with more time. When she got back from her trip I received this text:

"I don't know what I expected. But I didn't expect this."

I panicked a bit, thinking she was unhappy with the work but a few moments later, a second text came through:

"It looks amazing! I can't believe this is my room. I opened up the drawers and doors like you said to and I don't even remember how I had it before because this all makes so much sense. And the paintings! I never thought to put my father's paintings in here. I love it so much. This is better than I ever dreamed it could be. Thank you."

5

The Game Is On!

In Chapter 10 of my book *STOP BUYING BINS*, I introduced you to Priya, Tom, and their blended family. By way of quick recap, Priya and Tom have five kids between them, a six-bedroom house, and almost two of every small appliance on the market since they each came to the marriage from their own home. When they called me in, it was to introduce some order to the chaos so they could focus on being a family. And what a family—one of the warmest and closest families I have ever had the pleasure of working with. They just needed to get their stuff and systems running like a well-oiled machine.

One of the areas in their home that needed a reassessment was the family room—a room that could not be measured by the typical use of the average family. On the weekends, this seven-member household, all of whom were huge fans of both professional and college football (Tom played college football for the Air Force Academy), were camped out in the family room watching whatever game was on. Add to that a collection of friends with an open invitation to stop by, and it was wall-to-wall people nearly every Saturday and Sunday.

The current setup of the room made it difficult to accommodate everyone. Plus, in my opinion, the entire room was positioned facing in the wrong direction. If you read my last book, the back wall in their family room led to the garage and it was there that I designed a mudroom area to contain their comings and goings of coats, shoes, backpacks, etc. At the time, I had an additional reason for making that placement suggestion—I really wanted to rearrange the family room the "right" way.

What exactly qualifies as the right way? Well, let's talk about the form and function of a family room.

PRACTICALITY. What makes the most practical sense for a family room?

- Comfortable seating to support your entire family at once.
- Sufficient flat surfaces for placing cups, mugs, and plates of food if you are allowing such.
- Possibly a table for board games and puzzles if that's your thing.

- Accent lighting for individual activities (reading, crafts) in addition to quality overall room lighting (ideally overhead).
- Sufficient storage for entertainment equipment and accessories.
- Sufficient electrical outlets to support electronics.

The practicality of a family room comes down to accommodating the entire family and providing for each activity performed in the room. If you don't watch TV, the whole space can be devoted to whatever common pursuit you as a family enjoy. Just make sure it offers the whole family the opportunity to enjoy it together.

EFFICIENCY. Now that we have the practicality in place, how do we make and keep this heavily used space efficient? Here are a few more questions to ask yourself.

- Does every seat have a clear view of the TV?
- If you are allowing food and drink, does every seat have a flat surface within reach to place plates and glasses?
- Do the electronics, or at least the dreaded cords, tuck away? Are they neat and gathered or a tangled mishmash?

- Do you have storage for games, crafts, gaming equipment, that is sufficient to keep it neat and ideally hidden?

In the last 15 years or so, movie theaters have come around to the idea of the comfort-of-home experience: chairs that lean back with leg support, multiple cubbies for cups and concessions, restrooms in the theater for minimal disruptions. Some even have seat-side waiter service, not unlike calling to mom in the kitchen "can you bring me a drink?" Consider upgrading your family room to rival that comfort-of-home experience the theaters are attempting to woo you with. It's not as difficult as you'd think, *and sodas don't cost $7.95 a piece.*

ROUTINE. This room gets used and maybe even slightly abused. Keeping it neat comes down to some simple systems and helpful habits.

- If you take it out, put it back. This goes for game consoles to puzzle boxes to grandma's granny square throw. Once you are finished using it, put it back where it came from.

- If you bring it in, take it out. It's a meme on social media for goodness sake; you know that photo of all the mugs and glasses in the family room and nothing in the kitchen cabinets when you go for one. If it doesn't live in the room, don't leave it in the room.

- If you move it, find its home when you're finished. Remotes/clickers/flippers whatever you call it in your house, if you are the one doing the channel surfing, when you are finished do not leave it to fall between the couch cushions where the next person cannot find it. Put it back in the designated location, front and center and visible to all.

- A room that gets this much use needs weekly care at a minimum. Vacuum rugs and upholstery, dust electronics, clean surfaces of crumbs and cup rings. Always check couch cushions— *both my dogs liked to hide (excuse me, store) dog treats for later in the couch. Yikes! Enough said.*

Obviously enough, a room that takes a punch like the family room needs to be continuously maintained to ensure more rounds in the ring. The more care you put into it, the longer it will work for you. Abuse and disrespect it and it will look tired and worn in no time.

DECOR. For a room with so many requirements, function is key. Keep decor simple, comfortable, functional, and easy to clean. And limit extra decor and breakables.

- Whether you opt for sectional sofas or individual overstuffed chairs, always have a visual flow as well as physical flow around furniture. Shuffling in sideways between pieces of furniture is not practical.

- Big furniture does not always equal more seating. You can't expect someone to sit on the gap between two cushions. If you need to accommodate more derrières than the three spots provided with a standard three-cushion couch, consider a bench cushion sofa. Likewise, the chaise section of a sectional sofa is meant for one person, two if you want to get snuggly. But for everyone else, if you want to put your feet up when you're bingeing Netflix, make sure you have pieces to serve that purpose. One long ottoman or multiple foot rests; you get the picture.

- Nothing makes a room look less harmonious than lots of stuff everywhere, all out in the open. Have some kind of closed storage option for all gaming or entertainment equipment (that includes both the electronics and the accessories). Same goes for board games or crafts. And if you like to cuddle up under blankets while watching your favorite films, have some storage options for those too. Then once you're done using them, everything goes back into its home.

- It's a family room. Keep it simple and stick with that theme. Family photos, either tabletop or wall hung. Accent lamps that are task specific. Some type of holder for remotes. Coasters for drinks. Throw pillows that don't take up more room than people on a sofa. There is already so much going on in this space. No need to add much more.

* * *

Priya and Tom's house was laid out like a traditional center hall colonial, even if this particular home was at least twice the average size. Upon entering the front door through the impressive two-story foyer, straight through to the back of the house was the kitchen. If you stood in the center of the kitchen facing out to the backyard, the formal dining room would be to the far left, the eating area of the kitchen would be to the right, and beyond that, the massive family room sat sunken two steps down. Even though it was huge, it was a good deal longer than it was wider, making furniture arrangement tricky.

Stepping down into the family room, the door to the garage and the new mudroom area ran down the right-hand wall. Opposite that, the wall to the left had two sets of beautiful palladian windows facing the backyard. The wall straight ahead was a blank canvas, but as I said, the room ran longer rather than wider so that bare wall was confusing from a furniture placement perspective. Additionally, it had no outlets.

NOTE: Interior designers and architects, when you are laying out a room, would you please consider how a family will use their space when determining size or where to put outlets? I'm not sure what you expected would go on this huge blank wall clearly meant for a TV.

The first time I entered this room, it felt immediately awkward since the furniture all faced away from the windows as if these cushy characters had their backs to the audience. The entertainment center had been positioned where I eventually installed the mudroom area so at present, the TV was positioned in front of the cubbies like a freestanding room divider. The whole situation screamed discomfort, which is the exact opposite of what you want a family room to say.

We were working with the following: a 65" flatscreen TV on a large entertainment center console table, two side units which could be separated, a bench seat sofa/chaise sectional, two overstuffed armchairs, two matching footstools, a large rectangular tufted leather coffee table/bench, two old dining tables each with four dining chairs, AND just about every gaming system on the market. This was a family that enjoyed being together in one grand space—playing, eating, working. In my mind, I wanted to give this spacious room some fine-tuning and focus. So how exactly did I get there?

* * *

I gave Priya, Tom, and the kids a bit of homework. **They were to:**

- **Remove all dirty dishes, trash, homework, etc. and put these items where they belong.**

- **Go through all DVDs/CDs etc. and purge what no longer serves, then immediately drop at a donation center.**

- **Put all broken electronics either in the trash or in the car to be taken to a repair shop.**

- **Separate all gaming equipment by gaming system. Leave these piles out for me to organize. Purge as needed. Add to the donation collection.**

- **Do the same for craft supplies and board games/puzzles. (Remember that dried out glue and puzzles with missing pieces are NOT for donation. Please trash.)**

- **Vacuum all upholstery thoroughly.**

With seven people all shouting out "on it," "got it," "doing it now," I knew I'd be leaving the situation in good hands.

Next morning, donning a construction back brace, I got to work on the first big move of the day—the entertainment center. It separated into three pieces, but even still, it was heavy! My idea was to place the entertainment center between the palladian windows, opposite where it was currently. If you are not familiar with palladian windows, the easiest way to describe them is three typical windows side by side with an arched window above the center window. This room had two of those with blank wall space between them. *Now, truth be told, I was holding my breath that this huge piece of furniture would fit since my entire design hinged on flipping this room, and…I had forgotten to take measurements. I was up all night devising alternatives if it blocked part of the windows.* "Whew, it will fit," I said the next morning, retracting my tape measure and wiping my brow with a dramatic flare.

"You know what? I said to Tom last night, 'Bonnie is good! She didn't even have to take measurements to know it would fit.'" Priya was laughing while she winked at me.

"I knew it would fit. I just wanted to double check," I said, giving her a cute cherub look.

Slipping a set of furniture sliders under the feet, I glided the console table across the carpet to the other side of the room, leaving it a bit away from the wall. I had lots of cords to deal with when we got to that part. Next were the side units which I slid to sit on either side. Now for the real magic.

* * *

I believe to my core that there is never just one way to decorate a space. *There's not just one way to do anything in life while we're at it.* **However, there is something to be said for logical furniture placement that allows for the best overall use of a room, in addition to ideal energy flow (à la feng shui).** Principles like living room seating positioned into conversation vignettes, or not pushing the side of any bed bigger than a twin against a wall, and always closing the lid on the toilet seat before flushing. *But I digress.* Blocked walkways, visual barriers, feeling like you have to bend your body around obstacles, these are all furniture placement issues to be avoided. Even so, sometimes you are only left with one way to make it work.

"Does it really matter? Seems like moving the furniture is going to be a lot of work for nothing," Tom said, gathering his things to head out for the day.

"Just wait, Tom. You'll walk in here later today and even if you don't see a difference, you're going to feel one. Promise."

"Well, I trust your judgment, Bonnie," and with that, he kissed his wife and off he went.

"What's next?" said Priya.

"You go and start your day. You mentioned a phone call you had to make, right? I got everything handled here."

"Okay. Well, call me if you need me." And she went to her home office upstairs.

I looked back at this room of furniture, took a cleansing breath, and began pushing pieces into place.

* * *

Let me take this moment to backtrack a bit. This family had done a phenomenal job of clearing out and sorting this room. But if you don't have multiple elves working for you overnight, **here is how to handle the task on your own:**

1. **Remove anything that has a home in another room.** *I'm thinking errant socks peeled off while watching TV.*

2. **Downsize all electronics.** Trash what doesn't work. Gather what you will be donating or selling. Make piles of what's left separated into sets that work together. *I told the kids that I know next to nothing about gaming systems, so if they didn't want me storing the Nintendo*

Switch games with the PlayStation 5 controllers, they'd better do the sorting for me.

3. **Take this opportunity to clean.** Pull out all the attachments on your vacuum and go to town on the upholstery, the draperies, the carpeting.

4. **Begin moving the furniture to their new locations.** Start with the biggest pieces and work your way down to accessories. *In this home it was the entertainment center first, followed by the upholstered furniture, and then the remaining pieces.*

Here's where I jump ahead so you can get the big picture.

5. **Once the furniture is in place, make adjustments by actually using the pieces.** Are the ottomans close enough to the couch to put your feet up? *Maybe that's just a short girl problem. I'm sure 6'4" Tom never had to consider such a thing.*

6. **Move onto organizing your extras.** You will need bins. *I get such a kick out of people saying to me "but you said stop buying bins!" I said stop buying them, I didn't say stop using them when needed.* In some sort of square container,

line up your games (names visible), wrap cords around controllers or rubber band them and place them in the box next to the games.

7. **Repeat steps #2 & #6 for craft supplies or any other category of assorted things you use in the room.** You will need bins again.

8. **Now, you can go back in and layer decor—** pillows, throws, wall art, framed photos. Keep it all to a minimum. *Remember this is a room that gets a lot of wear and already comes with a lot of stuff. No need to add much more to the mix. My suggestion is add only what makes the space more comfortable—whatever that means to you.*

* * *

When you strip any space down to the basics, what you are left with is all that matters. Things will naturally get out of hand from time to time, but the framework will always be underneath. And that was my goal here, to get to a clear framework this family could always work back to. **Let's take a look at how I completed this room:**

1. **Since we had moved the entertainment center, it was time to move the couch/chaise**

sectional. I dragged it around in a circle to face the TV and positioned the couch portion squarely center to the screen. Then I dragged it back a few feet to allow for three important aspects: distance from the TV, visual walkway from the kitchen, sufficient space in the mudroom area.

a. Yes, you want to be able to see the TV. No, you don't want to go blind watching it. There are charts online to give you some guidance. For this 65" TV, the suggestion is between 8' and 13.5' from the screen.

b. Visual walkways are more important than you might imagine. When you enter a room, your eyes assess the easiest path to your destination. If you have to snake around furniture, you are unconsciously met with an uncomfortable feeling of either being trapped or fatigued. Removing visual obstacles is essential to the all-important natural flow of energy. Once I had moved the sectional back to 8 feet, I took note that I still had three feet of good space to back up more and still have a clear visual as well as a physical walkway from the kitchen.

c. But remember, I had built that back wall into a mudroom area. Moving the sectional back to 11 feet from the TV made the mudroom space just a bit snug. So I moved it forward this time 6 inches to find the sweet spot. Done.

2. **With the two biggest pieces in the room in place, everything else could now be built around them.** Since the chaise portion ran down the right side of the sectional, I placed the two armchairs side-by-side and at a right angle to the left of the couch. All the pieces then created a U-shape in front of the TV. The large rectangular tufted leather coffee table served as both a table (I added a flat surface tray for that purpose) and foot rest for the sofa and the armchairs.

3. **Not wanting to clutter the space with additional pieces, I placed the footstools that had been used previously with the armchairs, behind the sofa.** The idea being that if extra seating was needed, they could be pulled out but not be part of the usual arrangement. In the meantime, they were in an ideal spot to be used as part of the mudroom area.

4. **The two old dining tables used for crafts and games gave me a tremendous idea for my signature piece.** The two tables were both

solid wood and the same size square (one was a solid square, one was an extension table that had no leaves), but they were not the same height. With Priya's permission, I took the tables with me for a surprise project. Since she was planning to donate them anyway, she didn't mind at all. *I assured her she would love it because it was not only what the space needed, but also would be the perfect expression of her blended family.*

NOTE: So what did I do, you ask? With the help of a DIYer friend, I took the tables to his house to use his space, tools, and expertise. I wanted to add wood balusters to each of the four legs on the shorter table so the two tables would become the same height. Then I wanted to secure the extension table so it would no longer open. Once secured, I added two large heavy duty sliding latches to the underside of one side of each table so they could attach to each other. After some adjustments, a light sanding, and a quick varnish stain, I even surprised myself with how beautiful it turned out. *A true blending of two families into one!*

5. **When I returned with the tables, I needed Priya's help bringing them into the house. She thought I had just refinished them and was already happy with that outcome. Once I showed her the tables actually slotted**

together and explained my reasoning, she cried. *I have to be honest; I kinda love when my clients cry happy tears.*

6. **The eight wood chairs were a melange of upholstered seat cushions and various styles amassed from different homes. I cleaned them with lemon oil and reupholstered them to create some continuity with the table.**
   I liked the individuality of the chairs being different—*again, just like this family.* But I also wanted them to coordinate with the room. I brought some fabric samples I had left over from past projects, asked Priya to pick one, and with an electric staple gun in hand *(my aforementioned favorite toy),* I reupholstered them. Now, placed around the table, it looked like a true bespoke designed piece for games, crafts, and meals.

NOTE: This is an organizing book, not a decorating book, but it's also about using what you have instead of purchasing new. The cycle of buying creates the cycle of clutter, which more times than not leads to disorganization. If we just tried to make do with what we have, we wouldn't "need" to keep buying more. More is a slippery slope to too much.

7. **Earlier in this chapter, I mentioned putting gaming accessories in a bin.** The center console table was wide enough for the 65" TV and two different game systems which sat on either side of the TV console table top. Underneath the table top was a large drawer, big enough to hold all the accessories for both systems. I kept these items in bins but removed the lids. This way, if someone were to open the drawer, they could reach in and pull out just what they needed or the whole bin at once.

8. **On either side of the center console table were the two shelving units.** One unit had two shelves with two drawers below. The other had four cubbies (two over two) over four cubby cabinets with doors.

    a. The family had already sorted through their board games and puzzles but I took them a step further. Games with boxes in good condition were put immediately in the drawers. Any loose pieces without an original box or with a beat-up box, were put into a gallon-sized ziploc bag as a set and laid in the drawer bound to the playing board with a jumbo binder clip. Anyone who wanted to play a game or do a puzzle could easily find one looking down into the drawer. *No more giving up on a game because no one wanted to take the time to find all the pieces.*

b. The family had already sorted through their crafts supplies to downsize. Now it was time to organize. I divided the supplies into activities: scrapbooking and paper crafts, knitting and yarn art, and finally paint/markers/crayons. When it comes to your own home, sort according to your interests. Each group of materials in each category was bagged or gathered together in some way: small items in snack-sized or sandwich-sized ziploc bags, large binder clips to hold stacks of paper together. Then assigning each doored cubby to one of the craft activities, I placed the items in shoebox-sized bins and placed them inside. Anyone who wanted to make a craft, only needed to open that cabinet and pull out the bin. *No more digging through a big assortment in the corner of the room.* The last of the four-doored cubbies I used for large craft supplies—*like that gallon jug of white glue that never seems to run out.*

c. On the shelves above the drawers, I folded several individual lap throws that had been lying over the sofa and chairs and stacked them there. *Neater and nicer looking than having them strewn around the room and still within easy access when needed.*

d. The top two cubbies I used for large coffee table books. *No need to have them on the actual coffee table. That space needed to be kept clear for extra seating.* And the lower two cubbies were for DVDs *(which for the moment I was letting the family keep, even though they no longer had a working DVD player)*.

With the work complete, I stepped into the kitchen to do my **fresh-eyes approach**—which means I left the room and came back in to see if anything was off. It flowed perfectly and it felt like everything was where it was supposed to be, *not like it had been that first time I saw it*. I did the same thing coming in from the garage through the mudroom area. Again, easy and accessible. I was completely happy with this space.

CLEANING & MAINTENANCE

A family room is easily one of the top most used spaces in a house, and the more people who use it, the more regular cleaning and maintenance has to be done. My advice here is simple: **maintain it daily, clean it weekly. Here are some habits the whole family can share in:**

- **If you brought it in, take it out.** A cup of coffee, math homework, hair ties. It doesn't matter what it is. If it doesn't belong in the room, it doesn't belong in the room.

- **If it gets pulled out, put it back.** That applies to your Game Boy, your Cricut system, the latest Grisham novel. It needs to go back to its home at the end of you using it.

- **If you sat on it, fluff it.** Easy enough. *Those throw pillows working their way into the gap between cushions don't belong there.*

- **If you aren't finished but are coming back to it, consolidate it.** Puzzles and that never-ending game of monopoly come to mind. Neaten the table top, straightening the space, don't hog it all.

- **Vacuum the rug/carpet and upholstery weekly.** If you have sheddy pets, you may want to do it twice a week.

- **Dust the electronics weekly.** They are literally dust magnets.

- **Wipe down the table as often as it gets used.** Drips of glue and water glass rings as well as food crumbs need to be nipped in the bud as soon as possible.

- **Consistently downsize and recycle your equipment, etc.** I'm thinking of those DVDs with no way to be played but also any video games that never quite make it into the rotation.

- **Make repairs as needed.** Don't let that tear in your upholstery go too long without being mended either by a professional or DIY. Something small will turn into something much bigger in no time and then you are looking at replacing instead of repairing.

DECOR JUST FOR PRIYA, TOM, & FAMILY

The furniture had been positioned properly in the room, taking into account enough seating as well as foot support for each family member should they all be watching TV at the same time. There was also enough seating around the newly upcycled table that if they all wanted to play a game together, they could. The electronics had been installed and the cords had been bound with zip ties behind the entertainment center out of sight. The gaming systems were set up and the accessories were in open bins inside the drawers just below the table top. All with easy visual access when playing but out of sight when not. The side units were filled with games and crafts supplies, folded lap throws, art/coffee table books, and lined-up DVDs, all organized and easily accessible for use.

So it was just the final flourishes left to be handled.

- Throw pillows. Check.
- Plants on the top of the entertainment center *(sitting on boot trays so any water wouldn't ruin the wood)* all loving life with the sun from the palladian windows. Check.
- New shades Priya had installed, blocking out any sun that made it difficult to see the TV at certain times of the day. Check.
- On the center of the table, not wanting to add too much knowing that each time the table was used it would have to be moved, I laid a long metal tray and added a few scented candles I found in the kitchen.
- The last piece in this family room was one that made me cry. *Get the tissues ready:*

Tom had given Priya as a birthday gift a few months before two 20"x24" framed family photos from their wedding. One was a very formal family photo of all of them posed under an arbor and in the center the bride and groom. It was truly beautiful.

But I'm not a fan of staged formal photos. I never have been. I love photos that capture a real moment. Apparently Priya felt the same and Tom knew it, because the other framed photo was a candid shot. It was a photo of the family all hugging and smiling and looking up in awe at the fireworks on display to close out their special day. Faces lit by the fireworks and nearby ambient light, each one of them a picture of pure joy. Yes, hair was out of place and part of outfits had gone missing. Priya's hair was down from her updo. One of the boys had a school sweatshirt on with his bowtie. But it was real and it was happiness personified. And it was a perfect reflection of this wonderful and warm family, which made it perfect for this family room.

Priya had planned to hang them both in the living room but I persuaded her to let me use the candid shot. I hung it in its striking gold frame in the center of the wall behind the table so you could see it from anywhere in the room—a room made for a family.

* * *

Epilogue: Priya called me a few days later. On the day I finished the family room, she was watching TV on the couch waiting for Tom to get home. He was working late and didn't get home until nearly 10pm.

Tom: (walking into the house from the front door) Hey, who's still awake? (walking through the house to where he heard the TV).

Priya: Just me. I'm watching TV. Come join me.

Tom: (flopping down on the couch next to Priya, letting out a deep breath) I am so tired. It feels good to be home. It feels really comfy in here. How did you get the kids to clean up their shi—Holy cow! (bouncing up from the couch) This room looks awesome!

Priya said she laughed and laughed.

I told him he would feel it!

6

Mommy, Can I Have Friends Over for a Playdate?

I have such fond, if not also slightly neurotic, memories of my daughter's playrooms. There was a space in her bedroom, a space in the family room, and a dedicated playroom in the finished basement, which was a huge selling point for the family who bought the house from me. *I actually heard the three-year-old squeal delightedly when she saw it. Nothing makes me happier than knowing that the house my daughter grew up in now has a new young family to love and care for it.*

Blame it on being a stay-at-home mom, blame it on having only one child, or especially, blame it on being someone who loves life in neat rows, but every night after my daughter fell asleep, I would reset her play spaces back to looking like the window displays of FAO Schwarz. Every book categorized and back on the shelf. Every crayon back in the box in ROYGBIV order.

Every smiling plush puppy facing up out of a basket, ears tucked, paws under chins, awaiting the return of their tiny human the following morning.

But let's be serious here, I am a person who craves order and life-at-right-angles with one child who is a whole lot like me so being able to keep things organized when she was little was far easier than most. This chapter is going to be about how I kept it together and how you can too, if ever-so-slightly less intensely. I'm going to talk about day-to-day play systems, rotating in and out "fresh" toys, and even kids' playdate ideas. And I'll make every attempt to make sure everything I write falls under the umbrella of organizing and not spin off into parenting advice because this book isn't about that *(even though I have LOTS of opinions on that subject too—haha)*.

PRACTICALITY. Can a playroom be practical? In a way, yes.

- Nooks within a room keep things neat. A nook to read. A place for crafts. A nook for music. A place for building. You get the idea.
- Creating a designated play space by definition means it is meant for play. So EVERYTHING must be kid-friendly.
- Prepare for messes by expecting them. It takes the pressure off.

- Don't expect perfection. Strive for some semblance of order instead.

Keep in mind the kid. Are they engaged? Are they having fun? Are they safe? Can you (and eventually with their help) straighten up in mere moments? And can you achieve a certain level of precision in the process for that toy store look? There are ways to achieve all of this and not spend hours doing it.

EFFICIENCY. You can't get the look without laying the foundation for keeping it that way. The efficiency comes from keeping it simple. And yes, you will need bins (or baskets, or containers, or toy boxes, etc.).

- Make cleanup easy by working toward order, not perfection.
- Practice makes close to perfect.
- Clearview bins and ziploc bags of all sizes are your best friends.
- Most importantly, limit what is available at any given time.

Remind yourself that whatever you did the night before to get it back to square one will be drastically altered once a day of play has begun. Don't stress the small stuff. Your child is learning through play AND messes. It's all part of the same growth.

ROUTINE. Like the family room in the last chapter, this space gets used and abused. And the same routine rules apply.

- If you take it out, put it away.
- If you bring it in, take it out.
- If you move it, put it back.
- Daily tidying, weekly cleaning.
- Model good tidying skills so eventually your children clean up after themselves. *This is a teachable moment to learn respect for your things; it's not about rigid compliance to the floor plan.*

No one likes to clean but everyone likes the results. Make cleaning up easy and fun—for both you and your kids. If you're in a time crunch or you're playing the "how fast can we clean up" game, getting whatever it is in a bin is better than nothing at all. *Suggestion (which of course you can take or leave): don't correct them during cleanup; wait until the task is finished and then, together, check your work and make corrections, thus setting them up to learn how to not only see the problem themselves but self-correct. And no one, not even a three-year-old, wants to hear "no, not like that." That's a setup for "then you do it" if ever I heard one.*

DECOR. I'm going to make this one easy. None.

- If you can't play with it, can't get it dirty, might break it, or it can be harmful, what is the point?

- The theme is kid; toys are decor enough. So is baby-proofing. Safety is an aesthetic in my proverbial book.

- If you'd like to decorate, use unframed posters. The chance of knocking a framed piece of art off the wall is great—*been there.* Don't risk it. And while you're at it, don't use tacks, use poster putty or Command Strips. *Believe me, finding a tack by way of bare feet is worse than finding a Lego.* I also like "working" wall decor like magnet boards, white boards, chalkboards, all at kid height. They can be used for play as well as learning.

- Another decorating option, hang items from the ceiling. Kites, fairy lights, Calder-esque mobiles, as long as your kid is not one to try to pull them down.

- Lastly, little furniture. Play tables with framed out edges so toys don't fall off. Little table and chairs. A tiny reading couch that folds out to a daybed. *Man, I love kids' spaces!* A giant word of caution though. They will outgrow these items so don't go overboard outfitting the space.

When I was pregnant with my daughter, I was often asked what the theme in her nursery would be. At the time, not knowing she was going to be a she, I always said the same thing: KID. The theme is kid. Kids come with so much stuff I felt being nonspecific lent itself to one less decision for my anxiety-ridden mommy brain. More importantly, back then I would have totally lost it if I were to choose a theme and someone gifted us something that didn't "go". *If I chose pastel-colored Peter Rabbit and someone gave me a crib mobile with primary-colored jungle animals, I would have been silently hyperventilating. I'm so much less crazy now.* Not having a theme is a theme and practically guarantees that everything "goes" if it's meant for a kid. I realize we are not talking about a nursery in this instance, but that's even more reason not to have a theme in a play area. It's an even bigger mish-mash of things. No need for grand decor. Storage and neatness are all the design you need.

* * *

I love children's space—bedrooms, playrooms, classrooms. I love creating spaces for children to grow in and be inspired by. These little people are growing into themselves, and their caring adults need to give them the best chance at finding their individual sparks.

"Enough Bonnie! Stop waxing poetic and tell me how to fix this menagerie."

Of course. Here we go. **As always, we are going to break it down into small, digestible parts. Starting with the all-important purge.** But we're going to go beyond just downsizing. We're going to discuss the lifetime cycle of downsizing so your kids learn what you did not about holding onto extra. Our children are working from a clean slate. This is an opportunity to break our own ties to our stuff by not passing on the gathering gene. Teaching them how not to put undue value on possessions, or as important, respecting the possessions they have, will have them learning the priorities of family and generosity. I understand how difficult it is to get rid of toys, books, etc. that have barely had time to be used. It can be difficult for us when our children outgrow the things we are not ready to part with. I've witnessed many a mommy holding a toy that their child no longer plays with and saying aloud how much she misses those days, how they wish they could go back. So instead, they keep the item in memorial to the person their child once was, forgetting the person their child IS, guilting their child into holding onto something they never loved as much as the parent. It's a path fraught with sentimentality and faux value. And I'm not for a moment suggesting I have not been a party to it. I have my own "treasures" to prove it. But in this moment of clarity, let's all be realistic about what remains in a playroom—toys, books, etc. that our children need to GROW. There are some questions to ask yourself to get the ball rolling:

- **Do you have any unopened toys?** Perhaps your child just had a birthday and your friends and family were far too generous. Have your child pick 1-3 to open now and store the rest away. Every month or so, take a look at your back stock. Are there toys that could be worked into the rotation? Then by all means, do. Are there toys that your child has already outgrown or you know will hold no interest for them? Put them aside for now (options below). My point is this: Your child will likely never play with every toy they are given; they likely don't play with all the toys they have now. More will just be more for them and too much cleaning up for you. Options:
  → Hold for hand-me-downs.
  → Hold for gifts.
  → Donate to a children's organization throughout the year.
  → Donate to Toys for Tots at the end of the year.
  → You can also consign toys at a children's consignment shop and make back some piggy bank filler. Or sell them yourself either at a yard sale or online.
  → Or exchange them for a more suitable item. *I post this last because exchanging means you are still bringing more toys in—unless "Wendy Wets a Lot" is going back to Walmart in exchange for needed diapers.*

- **Do you have opened toys that are not being played with?** There will always be a favorite toy. That one special guy that collects stitches to keep them together while other toys collect dust. *Patches, an adorable floppy dog, has been my daughter's favorite since she was 18 months old. She's 20 now, and Patches is at college with her.* The favorites will remain favorites. But they're not all going to be given a place of honor. Watch which ones your child plays with consistently. Leave those in place. But as for the others, work them in and out of rotation (options below). Otherwise, what you'll have on your hands is "Baby's First Clutter." Options:
  → With younger kids, make it a game to present them with a toy that's not getting played with. If they show no interest, take it as a sign. They don't have the hoarding gene yet, so if they don't want it, they don't want it. Donate, gift, or sell.
  → With older kids, ask them point blank about the toys in question. Suggest maybe those toys they are not interested in could be donated to a thrift store or children's organization (check for any restrictions beforehand).
  → Make rotation and donation a habit by having your child donate 2-3 old toys for something from the new pile.

> → There is always the consignment or sell option too.
> → And if you have other younger children or plan to, no need to have all the toys out getting dusty and going unloved with your older child. Pack them away in a clear plastic bin *(I can't believe I'm saying that)*, remembering to remove batteries first, and bring them back out for the next little one in turn.

- **Is there too much of a good thing going on?** Crayons! I know your kids will never use up every crayon in the house. And how do I know this? Because I lived it. They are more likely to be lost in the car on your next roadtrip than fully used up. So if you have multiple boxes, pass some along. School supplies are always in need.

- **Anything broken or missing pieces is an automatic out, unless it's a favorite.** Then by all means, repair and save.

- **All the same principles apply to books, and sporting goods, and certainly clothes (you know the drill by now).**

* * *

We all want to give our children the best start in life and that includes giving them every opportunity to cultivate their as-yet-undiscovered talents. Sports, art, languages, math, whatever it is, there is a learning toy to go with it and an adult trying to make an impression upon a forming mind. Use this to your advantage as you create (or recreate) your play spaces by designing vignettes for each activity.

Regardless of the amount of space or rooms you have to devote to kids' play in your home, you can still create areas meant for separate activities. Consider how a preschool classroom is set up. There are no finger paints in the play kitchen and no books on the playground. Each classroom is set up into sections giving the child a choice of interests on that given day, in that given moment. With this in mind, **create spaces that are conducive to the activity performed there AND make it easy for cleanup at the end of the play.**

- **A space for reading.** Perhaps a bookcase or book bin where all the books are easy to see by their spine or cover. No need to put them in any special order other than size. Cushions, pillows, stuffed animals, blankets. And a good light source either from a lamp or window. This should be a quiet space for your child to sit and enjoy books, by themselves or as parallel reading. The value of children learning to love reading and storytelling is immeasurable. And providing them a space to explore books shows that reading is a priority in your family's life.

- **A space for art.** Ideally where goopy accidents are a given and cleanup is easy. Clear lidded bins with contents separated by item, ideally no larger than what your child can carry. A sink is a bonus. But even if you don't have these options, you can still provide for gooey arts and crafts with washable paints and glue, smocks or aprons, vinyl tablecloths, and even shower curtain liners under foot. Crafts for little ones should be supervised but otherwise uninterrupted. Letting children explore art supplies is one of the greatest joys to witness. Their uninhibited approach to using the materials is where true art comes from. And it doesn't take much. A bucket of puffy stickers, some crayons, and colored construction paper makes for a full afternoon of fun. Working on fine motor skills is a bonus.

- **A space for building.** A large open space ideally carpeted for crashes. A table top surface, preferably kid height, for smaller blocks like Legos. And bins, lidded or not, for each type of block. Kids are natural builders—just watch what they do with a paper cup and a plastic spoon at the beach. Lots of learning goes into building not the least of which is balance, as well as perseverance and problem solving.

- **A space for household maintenance.** Some of you are going to disagree with me on the gender roles behind this but I'm putting it in here just the same. This isn't a child-rearing book. It's an organizing book. And the point of all this is to teach our children, <u>all</u> children, how to keep things neat and orderly. How better to do that than with some real world, albeit small sized, practice. Kid cooking things, kid cleaning things, or just give them a pot and wooden spoon and a sponge. They can watch you and mirror along. A handheld vacuum is a neat "toy," as is folding laundry (small squares like washcloths are easy). Kids are amazing at mimicry (that's why dirty words are so easy to pick up). May as well teach them some practical things along the way.

There are at least a half dozen more spaces you can create for your kids based on your needs and their interests, but I think you can see where I'm going with it. And all of these spaces cultivate play and learning. **Now, how do you keep it neat once you've made it?**

* * *

At the top of my list of favorite toy company brands is ThinkFun. *(And no, I'm not getting a kickback for saying that.)* As the name suggests, they make strategic reasoning games for children and adults that are so entertaining and addictive they are hard to put down. But for me, what makes them so impressive is their packaging design. When you purchase one of their games, it comes with a fabric drawstring bag to keep the pieces and game board all together once you've opened it. It's ingenious! Barring these fabric pouches, **anything that comes in a box and has multiple pieces is better organized in a clear plastic zipper top bag. And here is why:**

1. You can see all the contents. No need to label the bag, but do remember to keep the instruction booklet.

2. Pliable bags make it easier to store in a toy box than rigid-sided boxes.

3. Easier too for small children to identify and sort into the correct bag on their own.

NOTE: If the playing board is large, there are XXL ziploc storage bags on the market. Or binder clip the bag with the pieces to the board. Does that sound like extra work? Consider how unattractive those beat-up boxes are and how often you have to tape the corners, then adding a binder clip doesn't sound all that bad, does it?

4. Continue the idea by collecting Lego kits together. Or forget the kits entirely and separate by color. Have your child handle the task of sorting. Not only is separating by color an early learning tool for young children learning colors and cleanup, but by separating kits, you encourage older kids to be creative in their design versus following the blueprints that come with the kit.

5. If you are not comfortable with all that plastic, there are quick tutorials online for making drawstring bags out of old linens or t-shirts, which is another way to upcycle what you already have without purchasing more. Even better.

6. If you want to take this all a step further, games are in one bin, blocks in another, dolls/action figures and their coordinating accessories in yet another. This has nothing to do with child development, and everything to do with keeping it neat.

What this all comes back to is organizing. **Organizing in its most basic form is sorting,**

separating, and storing neatly. And when do we learn these skills? In early childhood. **There are ways to teach these lessons without making chores a pain and each step builds upon the next as they grow:**

1. Clean up toys while your child is watching and explain your process as you go.

2. Engage your child by asking them to put piece A into bag A.

3. Have your child "correct" you by asking them if you are putting the right piece in the right bag.

4. Ask them to help you sort and bag the mix of items.

5. Always place bags back in their appropriate bin. Have them help. Have them "correct" you. "Correct" the work together.

6. Encourage your child to clean up after they have finished with an activity and before moving onto another.

Does this all happen magically every time? Of course not. But even 50% is better than not at all. And wouldn't it be lovely if while everything is being plucked up off the floor and thrown in a toy box, that it's in its own bag and not just at the bottom of a big pile of random detritus that will have to be weeded through to find it later? Bonus, they are learning the skills to do it themselves so it does not always fall to the caregiver.

CLEANING & MAINTENANCE

This entire chapter has been focused on cleaning and maintenance so I'm going to use this section to offer some tips I've picked up over the years. Things like:

- Has your child been snuggling with their stuffed animals when they are home with a runny nose? Those toys that can't be thrown in the washing machine to clean can be put in a plastic bag and stored in the freezer overnight to kill germs and dust mites.
- You know that hole in the bottom of rubber ducks to make them squeak? If you use those in the bath and they get water inside, mold will form. Use toys without accessible innards as bath toys.
- In our post-COVID lives, we want to be able to keep all toys sanitary. Gather Legos in a dishpan or bucket, cover with isopropyl alcohol, slosh around, rinse well with clean water. Leave to dry. Do not leave them too long in the alcohol since it may fade the color.

- Plastic toys and game pieces can be wiped down with a clean cloth dipped in soapy water or isopropyl alcohol. Wipe dry.
- Wipe out toy bins monthly. Even with pieces in individual bags, discards happen. So do dust and spiders.
- Vacuum play areas regularly. Wipe up food and drink spills right away. Same goes for art supplies—*unless, like me, you like the look of a paint-splattered work table.*

* * *

ADVICE FOR PLAYDATES

- Remove favorites from the mix beforehand and anything else your child does not want to share. *You don't like to share your favorite things either.*
- Limit the amount of toys available overall. *Less toys, less to tidy.*
- Encourage the same cleanup strategies with your child's guest. *Most parents will want to know their child was a good guest by helping to clean up.*
- Don't shy away from art projects, but do prepare for happy messes. *Smocks, towels covering upholstered chairs, tablecloths, drop cloths.*
- Weather permitting, outdoor play is a must. *And saves on indoor cleanup altogether.*

Since I usually wrap up these chapters with a section on decor and I've already said my bit about decor, I'll take this chance to offer up my version of a playdate idea for elementary school kids, that also encourages recycling, downsizing, and overall community. *Never too early to learn the lessons.*

"SWAPPING"

Book Swap: friends bring over three books, explain what the book is about and whether or not they liked it, and everyone goes home with "new" books to read.

Clothes Swap: friends bring over three pieces of clothing in a single category (shirts, sweatshirts, dresses, etc.), swap clothes, and do a fashion show with their "new" pieces.

Art Swap: friends bring over art supplies and share, making art for each of the friends there.

Unopened Toy Swap (Yankee Swap): friends bring unopened, gift wrapped toys, draw numbers, pick from the pile. You can add the "stealing" aspect if it's all in good fun.

I'm going to be honest here. When my daughter no longer needed me to plan playdates for her *(around the same time she stopped calling them playdates)* it was a little bittersweet. Party planning mixed with teachable moments is kind of a win-win for me. But I'm thrilled to say I apparently taught her, and by proxy her friends, well. They always had a plan of what they were going to do. It usually involved some creativity.

And they always cleaned up after themselves. And to this day, they continue to swap!

* * *

I will admit that this chapter is a little heavy handed on the stay-at-home parent hosting playdates scenario. But even if your child attends daycare, the room would likely be set up in the same way I described. The children would be encouraged to engage in one activity at a time as I suggest. And there would be cleanup time when everything went back into its rightful place as I recommend. At the end of the day, when the children go home, the teachers and aids would likely clean everything using the tips listed.

As important as learning to clean up after themselves, the children in all these scenarios learn respect for the things and people in their lives and not to treat either with disrespect. It's all combined with learning and fun and putting it all back to square one—and no one is screaming expletives because they stepped on a Lego.

7

I Don't Cook; The Kitchen's for Show

I lived through a 4-month kitchen renovation in my last house. I say "lived through" because it nearly killed me. When it was completed, not three days before we were hosting a big party with everyone from both sides of our large extended family traveling from New Jersey to Maryland, it was truly worth the stress and headache and anxiety-producing dust. But during, yes, it nearly killed me.

Gutting a kitchen to the studs has many benefits, but building your organized and user-friendly kitchen with what you have is not only achievable but also clearly cheaper *(and less likely to put you in the fetal position mumbling about backsplashes)*. All it takes is a bit of thinking things through in a way that makes the most sense for how you and your family use it. Whether you are a gourmet chef or a takeout-only kind of person there is a sensible way to outfit and organize your kitchen. And in doing so, you make your future cleaning up easier.

PRACTICALITY. As the most practical room in the house, the kitchen contents MUST be streamlined for what you use daily and what you use occasionally but regularly. I will explain further. Consider asking yourself some questions:

- Do you have a well-stocked pantry of food items you use? *There is a difference between a well-stocked pantry of go-to items you use in your meals and one filled with jars of peach pepper jam that came in a holiday fruit basket you received in 1994. Please empty the contents of said jar and wash thoroughly. Reuse the jar for leftovers or recycle.*

- Do you own small appliances and tools that you bought with the idea of using that are now taking up valuable space? *You know the ones. You purchased them when you had fleeting dreams of being a pastry chef because you were watching the "Great British Baking Show", but two years out they are all still in their boxes.*

- Do you have far more accessories than you need? *I'm questioning at this moment why I*

I Don't Cook; The Kitchen's for Show

myself have four cookie sheets when I consistently only use just the one that keeps getting washed and put back on top.

Simple enough. Only what you need and use and possibly a cupboard of items you use only occasionally but regularly, like that big lidded pot you use to cook Thanksgiving turkey once a year. But don't keep anything you don't use just because you think it is a necessity for a well-fitted kitchen. *I'll give you an example of what I mean: I am an avid coffee drinker. I have a coffee station in my kitchen. If you are not a coffee drinker, you do not need a coffee station. In fact, unless you regularly host coffee drinkers in your home, you don't even need a coffee maker.*

EFFICIENCY. The placement of tools and small appliances, frankly anything in your kitchen, is vital when setting up an organized kitchen. Focus on creating user-friendly spaces is a must since the occupants are multitasking with scorching hot pots and razor-sharp knives. Consider cooking processes and their possible issues when deciding what goes where.

- Store items where you use them. Coffee near the coffee maker. Cutting knives and cutting boards near each other and ideally on the counter area where you are likely to use them. But again, only if you use any of these things enough to make it necessary for them to be in plain sight every day.

- Place items used daily in easily accessible places. Items used rarely should be out-of-sight until needed. *You know that juicer you were totally into and then you ran out of produce and got out of the habit. What? Am I the only one?! Well, it no longer needs to be on the counter taking up space if it's not making morning carrot celery tonics.*

- Are the items stored in cabinets at an appropriate level for your height? *My fellow shorties know what I'm talking about. Standing mixers weigh up to 35lbs. They do not belong on a top shelf.*

Again, simple enough. **What you need where you need it so that when you need it, it's right there.** *If you need a step ladder to grab the salt while you're cooking, the salt needs to be moved. But while we're talking about it, your step ladder should always be handy—that's a tidbit for the 5'3" and under crowd.*

ROUTINE. Keeping your space clean involves more than moving the dirty dishes from the sink to the dishwasher, but once you're in the grove, your kitchen will never be out of control.

- Clean as you go. Every cooking competition show has that one judge who comments on the cleanliness of a contestant's station and how it translates to good cooking skills. So consistently put used pots, bowls, utensils in the sink while you work. Put ingredients away after you've used what you need. Keep counters clear so you can work.

- Organize and wipe down your refrigerator, cupboards, and pantry as you make your shopping list. Now that my daughter is away at college, my grocery shopping expeditions are monthly instead of weekly. To make my list, I go through all my food storage to see what I have and what I need, and while I'm at it, I do a quick wipe down with a soapy sponge. When I do a big spring clean annually, the work is next to nothing. *Another note: You know that ketchup bottle that gets clogged? Clean the cap after every few uses. You'll thank me later.*

- Wipe as you use, clean weekly. I'm not a fan of cleaning my stovetop. It has heavy cast iron grates that are cumbersome to wash in the sink. But if I do a quick cleanup after each time I cook something, it doesn't get as grimy and the heavy cleanings may go a few weeks.

Keeping your kitchen clean is a slippery slope, *quite literally if you fry food.* It needs care daily to keep up with grease and crumbs. Organizing helps to limit the amount of surfaces that need to be cleaned. Tips like not having all your small appliances out if you don't use them daily goes a surprisingly long way to keeping it clean as well as visually neat.

DECOR. The items you need in a kitchen are decor enough but if you have anything to add, keep it food friendly or washable.

- Wall color, backsplash, lighting, countertops, fixtures, cabinets—they are all decor.

- Keep added decor useful for food preparing or eating purposes. Mason jars with dried foods and spices or cloche-covered cake stands are what I mean by both decorative and useful.

- If you are going to add fabric items like window treatments and rugs, make sure to consider washability. Even if you are not in a habit of cooking foods that splatter, there is still the question of aromas getting stuck in fabrics.

When a kitchen is staged in a house that's being sold, what do stagers typically use to dress it? A bouquet of flowers or a bowl of fruit, maybe a decorative

I Don't Cook; The Kitchen's for Show

soap dispenser. A kitchen is already dressed with what you use every day. And by that logic, also already filled with items. No need for much more flare.

* * *

Before renovating my last kitchen, it was dysfunctional to say the least. The refrigerator was clear across the room, the double oven doors had carved a niche in the wall because they were installed too close, and don't even get me started on the gold medallion linoleum circa 1969. But even the best kitchens can be rendered useless without a bit of organizing and lifestyle systems.

Take for example my clients Jack and Miffy. They had a massive home custom-built just for them in McLean, VA, and every detail was considered including a huge professional-grade kitchen with all top-of-the-line appliances, granite countertops, custom-built farm sink, and Honduran mahogany floors. It was a showstopper in this already magnificent home. Oddly enough, no one in the family cooked.

"If you're going to build a custom house, you have to have a custom kitchen. Even if we only ever use it to heat up leftovers," Miffy quipped as she moved some papers off the center island and added them to a pile in the mudroom which led to a wing of the house where she had her home office. Both she and Jack were lawyers in DC. Empty-nesters with grown children and grandchildren, who most days left at 6am in an attempt to beat beltway traffic, then headed back home around 7pm when evening traffic had tapered off. In the middle, they had all three meals in the city. On weekends, they met up with friends or "the kids" hosted at their houses where they could spend time with the "grands." They rarely ate in their home except for the occasional catered event *(their usual caterers loved using their kitchen).*

You'd think that a room that got little to no use would always be in pristine condition. That wasn't the case for these two. The kitchen, sadly, became a mismanaged catchall of "kitchen essentials" and the comings and goings of two busy people who rarely spent any time in their home. The Saturday I saw it, there was dry cleaning hanging from a partially opened cabinet, and stacks of the Washington Post and The New York Times sharing space on the countertop with one brand name appliance after the next, all of which were collecting dust, some of which still had manufacturer stickers on them years after being purchased. I thought to myself that in a room this huge with so many cabinets, there had to be space to store these items away when they were not being used. I'm glad I didn't place money on that because I would have lost that bet. The cabinets were all filled as well. Piles of baking sheets and pans and cookie cutters all haphazardly placed, commingled with accoutrements from a lifetime of party goods. And lots of canned, jarred, and bottled food!

I Don't Cook; The Kitchen's for Show

"Can I ask you a blunt question? Why do you have so much food if it's just the two of you…and you never eat at home?" I asked, opening and closing cabinet doors as Miffy moved more piles of paper.

"Oh, you know, if we ever decided to just stay home, I could heat up a can of something or make some pasta with sauce. Plus snacks for when the kids visit."

Turning to her I said, "Ah got it. Well, what is your plan for this space, Miffy? What are your expectations for me?"

With that, Jack walked in from playing golf. He very graciously introduced himself, grabbed a bottle of water from the refrigerator, kissed Miffy on the cheek, and said, "Did you tell Bonnie?"

"I was just about to."

I looked from one to the other.

Then Miffy said, "Jack and I are retiring at the end of the year. Among other things, we are going to have to start feeding ourselves."

"We could just continue to eat out like we do now," Jack said with a wink to me as he walked into the butler's pantry/bar to pour himself a drink.

"Retiring, Jack! That means not spending money to eat out all the time." Miffy rolled her eyes and proceeded to wash an ashtray that must have been in the sink. Jack returned with his old fashioned in hand and a cigar in his mouth. She handed him the ashtray and a lighter in an effortless dance I was sure they had done hundreds of times.

"And you don't think that you burning food is going to mean double food bills when we have to go out anyway?"

"Who said I'm the one cooking?"

They both laughed and I had to smile being privy to the playful banter of a 41-year marriage.

* * *

The upside here was that since there had been no cooking in the house, nothing was dirty; perhaps just dusty. The downside was convincing, at least Miffy, that more than likely they would only be using the kitchen for breakfast and snacks since it was clear these two were looking forward to continuing to eat their meals out. To prove this point further, of the three weekend days I worked in their home, Miffy met her sister for lunch twice and Jack ate both breakfast and lunch at the club those same two days. They were not going to be using this kitchen much more than they had been but I was happy to create a user-friendly space they COULD use if they so chose.

Below was my three-day task list. I suggest that you keep a bucket of soapy water and a sponge on hand to clean out cabinets and drawers as you go. And please do not store away any small appliances without first making sure they are clean and food-free. *Bugs find everything.* Let's get started.

I Don't Cook; The Kitchen's for Show

DAY ONE
1. **Clear and clean a large surface area for sorting.** In this house, I used the large center island for this purpose. But the dining table is just as good.

2. **Prepare the trash can with a new bag and have a box ready for food donations.** I had a feeling there was going to be more expired food than donatable food so I also prepped two bins I had brought with me for recycling.

3. **Open all cabinets and drawers and pull out food, spices, drinks, snacks, anything ingestible.** Leave the refrigerator; that will be taken care of at the end of the project when you are cleaning.

4. **Sort. Consolidate. Check expiration dates.** This is an opportunity to tackle a number of tasks. From bringing all the same items together from their various locations, to consolidating two opened boxes of the same thing, to tossing that dusty can of tuna that expired before the label was required to note "dolphin safe." *(It's 1990, by the way.)*

5. **Pitch all expired foods.** If there are any in glass jars, empty, wash, and recycle. Pitch contents of boxes then recycle boxes. **Downsize food you are not likely to eat before expiration date.** Miffy had multiple boxes of cake mix with plans to bake for

and with her grandchildren. *When I say multiple, I'm saying a dozen plus.* I texted her to suggest she bag some to take to each family when she visited. For you, it may just be that you have second thoughts about using that jar of marinated mushrooms you had ideas of using, or you have one too many cans of soup. Whatever it may be, there is a food pantry in need near you.

6. **Before you begin putting the food back, consider where it should go.** This is an opportunity to make changes to how you work in your kitchen. Do you do mostly stovetop cooking? Consider moving your spices and oils near the stove. Are bread and cookie baking your thing? Place baking supplies near the island for the work space. Big on boxed cereal? Maybe they should go near the bowls and/or the refrigerator where the milk is kept.

7. **Wipe out the area where your supplies are going.** Soap and water does the trick. Wipe dry. Add or replace shelf liner if you'd like; shelf liner really comes down to the condition of your cabinets. New kitchen, no need for it but you may want to in order to keep it that way.

8. **Wipe down your cans, jars, and bottles with a damp rag before placing them in the predetermined location.** Not every food item in a pantry is

in its original state. Olive oils and other liquids that do not require refrigeration are ones that come to mind. They can get slick and sticky. Take the time now while you are involved in this process to clean them.

9. **When placing them back, labels out and large items in the back.** This has less to do with achieving that professional organizer signature look, and more about creating an ease to finding what you need. All you have to do is open a cabinet and everything is facing you. No more rummaging. Stack like canned items not on top of each other, but one behind the other so you can see all the different items you have. Larger items in the back makes sense so they do not block smaller items, but it also means it is more difficult to get out. Consider putting small items in a clear plastic bin that can be removed all at once for efficiency. An extra-efficient way to see all your items at once is to install rollout trays in your below counter cabinets, so there is no reaching for items in the back ever again. They are easy to install, come in various sizes, and are available at any home improvement store.

10. **Use airtight canisters when appropriate.** I am NOT big on removing the contents of items you just bought from the grocery store and reassigning

them into other containers. *It makes me insane to see eggs taken out of their ideal packaging and moved to clear plastic and then labeled. It came that way for goodness sake!* But some items, especially baking ingredients, are best stored in airtight containers not only for freshness, but also for less dust-like debris in your pantry and ease of use while baking. Items like bags of flour or confectioners sugar. Bags may be perfect for packaging from the manufacturer—less weight, less bulk—but that poof of fine granules every time the bag is folded gives me heart palpitations. Same applies to dry pet food. Use containers. *Yet another situation where I loosen my grip on the whole "stop buying bins" mantra.*

After all the food had been taken care of and back in more suitable conditions and locations, I washed out any containers that could be recycled. I collected the trash and put it out with the recycling. I gathered the box bound for the local church food pantry and put it in my car. Then I texted Miffy and Jack that I was leaving for the day and that the food items, with the exception of the refrigerator, were taken care of. Their homework was to open the cabinets and drawers and see how it all felt to them. Any changes we could discuss the next day when I arrived before they went out.

I Don't Cook; The Kitchen's for Show

DAY TWO

"It's all fantastic but I can't find the coffee. I'm sure it's in the 'right' place but I don't know where that is."

I laughed as I walked over to the cabinet near the kitchen sink (easy for filling the coffee maker) and opened the cabinet with the mugs, coffee canisters, and tea. "Yeah, that's on me. I haven't put the appliances in place yet. The coffee maker will go right here," I explained, touching the countertop. "Coffee and mugs above it." "I said it would be in the 'right' place, didn't I? Well, no bother, I'm heading out to meet a friend for coffee anyway." She grabbed her handbag and headed for the garage. "Text me if you need me. Good luck today. And thank you for all your help." Then she stopped and turned back to me. "It really does look fantastic. I'll be recommending you to this friend I'm meeting. She needs you badly!" And with that, she hit the remote to open the outside garage door and stepped out.

With Miffy and Jack out for the day, it was time to begin mine. Let's get moving. It's going to be a long day.

1. **Pull out all the dishes, bowls, glasses, and flatware. Anything you eat out of or off of.** In doing so, I found more than the center island could support so I began relocating drinking glasses to the butler's pantry, which also served as the bar connecting the kitchen to the formal dining room. There I found more glasses in an assortment of

styles and decided that this chaos had to be taken care of first. *Sometimes I get caught in a wormhole, because while a juice glass will serve for a few fingers of whiskey, it's just not what one does. I outfitted the bar first and the remaining glasses were brought back to the kitchen. For better or for worse, sidetracks happen.*

2. **Sort into categories. Check for damages.** Toss cracked or chipped glasses ASAP. Badly cracked or chipped plates, bowls, or mugs should be considered for the trash, especially if the crack is across the food surface and not just on the rim. *Cracks can capture food and grow God knows what. It's not worth it to hold onto them just to have a complete 12-piece set.* This is also a good time to consider more items to downsize for donation— *things like the promotional travel mug from a golf tournament you didn't wind up playing in but a coworker brought you back the next day anyway.*

3. **Take this moment to determine where everything should go.** This is yet another opportunity to make changes to the natural flow of your kitchen. Do you set the table before meals and eat family style, or do you plate meals and then serve them, or do you prefer a buffet? Then your plates should be closest to that working area, either

near your table, your cooking surfaces, or your buffet area/island.

4. **Wipe out the area where your supplies are going.** As noted earlier, soap and water is ideal. And while I may not have a preference for shelf liner, I do like to use a non-slip, rubber grip shelf liner under glasses.

NOTE: There is some discussion amongst the organizing community as to which way to place glasses on a shelf. One school of thought is to place the opening down to prevent dust from settling inside. The other is to place the base down because it is thicker which provides more stability.

I say there's a third option—consider the space. Take for example glass tumblers with angled sides. To fit them all on a shelf, you may have to do one up next to one down fitting them as close together as possible for the most efficient use of space.

5. **Regardless of your physical personal height, those items you use most should be on the lowest shelf within your cabinets.** I'm five feet tall so if it were up to me, everything would be in drawers below the counter or on a shelf right at eye level, but even if you are six feet or better, there is no sense in reaching up high for those everyday items. Put them front and center and in one row

across. That way you don't have to reach over anything either.

6. **Once everything is in place it's not necessarily set in stone.** Use the space over the next couple of meals and see if it feels right. Does where it is placed provide the most efficient use of your time and motion? *No, really! If you are constantly getting your colander from a cabinet across the room to use in the sink, that doesn't make much sense, does it?* And while you're at it, put the large mixing bowls there too. They fit together.

NOTE: Written into each of my client proposals is a two-hour "refresh" appointment approximately two weeks after the work has been completed. This gives the homeowners a chance to live with the systems in place and determine if it feels comfortable. It is of paramount importance to me that my clients can maintain the systems I've put in place for them. It's why I take the time to learn how they use their spaces during our initial meeting. I always consider how they live before devising a plan. In all the time I've done this work, I have only ever gone back to a home to make revisions once. These systems work!

In moving things out of cabinets and drawers to rearrange other items, I still had a full center island and tabletop of pieces to rehouse. I needed a break! I moved a chair to the center of the kitchen, sat down, and with all the doors and drawers open, I did some mental gymnastics moving things around in my mind's eye to calculate what goes best where. I still had pots and pans, baking supplies, serving pieces, cooking utensils, countless small appliances, and all the incidentals of a kitchen such as aluminum foil, plasticware, and birthday candles. For whatever reason, this project had my head spinning. I couldn't seem to focus even though this seemed like a dream job and fairly straightforward.

I rarely leave a project, but I decided to take a lunch break and get out of the house for some fresh perspective. As I sat with a sandwich on a bench outside a deli, it came to me—the reason I was lagging and uninspired with this project. I was approaching it wrong! Neither Miffy nor Jack was ever going to prepare elaborate meals in that kitchen on a regular basis and we all knew it. The best they might do is heat something up or sit down to takeout—AND THAT WAS FINE! Because instead of trying to think like someone who would use this kitchen to cook in, I could think of this kitchen as someplace to entertain in. It was party prep! I finished my sandwich and drove back to the house, newly inspired to tackle what was left.

7. **Collect all of one item category and start sifting.**
   For a couple of non-cooks they certainly had a lot of everything. I just jumped in with pots, pans,

and Pyrex. I cleaned out the cabinets beneath the cooktop and began matching lids to pots, nesting the lids handle upside down inside each one. You could stack your pots inside one another like nesting dolls, the largest lid of which sits handle down in the top pot, and then slide the other lids alongside, BUT I find that cumbersome in practice since every time you need a pot of a specific size, you have to rummage through all of them. If you have the room, having each pot with its corresponding lid and then stacked by twos or threes depending on the size of your storage is easier to manage. Bakeware generally used for cooking like Pyrex or Corningware gets stacked inside each other and stored near the wall ovens.

8. **Move onto another category and do the same. Let's talk about cooking utensils—rubber spatulas, wooden spoons, metal spatulas, whisks, etc.** The two schools of thought are on the counter or not. Surprisingly enough, I'm an on-the-counter advocate; right next to the stove. *It seems contrary to my clear surfaces rule but hear me out.* The single motion of grabbing a rubber spatula while you are cooking eggs on the stove is far more efficient than having to find it in a drawer. Plus, corralling them all in some decorative pottery crock or stainless steel caddy is a chance to add that functional decor I mentioned at the top of this chapter. Those

who prefer their countertops bare and their utensils hidden, of course may use a nearby drawer; sectioned drawer organizer a must. Having your utensils in a drawer also prevents your utensils from getting day-to-day dust and grime from being out in the open. I combat that by throwing them all in the dishwasher, including the containers, every couple months.

9. **Baking supplies next.** Nest baking sheets, cooling racks, and muffin tins and stand them on their side like books on a shelf. Hold trays in place with containers holding items like cookie cutters, piping tips, food coloring, rolling pins, offset icing spatulas, whatever you have on hand for baking that's on the small side and fits in a lidded box or bin. Pie dishes, loaf pans, nested and stacked on a separate shelf along with your canisters of flour, sugar, brown sugar, etc. Anytime Miffy or Jack wanted to bake with the grandkids, it was all in one place under the work surface of the island. *P.S. feel free to discard anything that has so much baked-on black crud that it is embedded in the surface. You likely would have passed it over for a cleaner one anyway.*

10. **During all the moving and sorting of items, most of the small appliances found their way to the kitchen table.** I wiped down the countertops

and began plotting out where things would go. The coffee maker was first, placed in its appropriate location near the sink and under the cabinet where I had previously put the coffee, tea, and mugs. Next to it, I chose a serving tray from the assortment to hold sugar, a bowl of non-dairy creamer cups, and other related items. On the opposite side of the stovetop from the utensil crocks, I set the toaster. I figured by the amount of crumbs in it that it was one of the items that got regular use. After cleaning it out, I plugged it in, in its new home. I decided to leave the wildly heavy standing mixer staged on the island to be used for baking. The waffle maker, the hand mixer, the blender, the immersion blender, the smoothie blender, the electric wok, the rice cooker, the food processor, the panini press, and the ice cream maker were all dusted, their accessories placed in zip-top bags, and placed in lower cabinets at the far end of the kitchen.

I left a note for Miffy to go through the cabinets again overnight and seriously consider gifting some of her beautiful unused appliances to her children or her friends. They were high-quality tools that she wasn't using. I wrote that I'd be back in the morning to handle the last piles—serving pieces and incidentals—and the butler's pantry which I was adding to my task list at no extra charge since it was really part of the kitchen.

She texted me that evening: "I don't remember buying this blender stick thing? *It doesn't look like something that should be in the kitchen...if you get my meaning?* Okay, I'm calling the kids now to see what they want. See you tomorrow."

DAY THREE

It was my last day on this project and I was ready to wrap it up with a bow. Quite literally, since I had brought a bouquet of fresh flowers as the final flourish on this project.

"Good morning, Bonnie! I hope you know, you may be responsible for single-handedly turning Miffy into a cook. If it were up to me, we'd eat out every meal but she's insisting that you did all this work to make the kitchen usable, she's not going to let it go to waste," Jack said, pulling on his golf visor and grabbing his car keys from the hook by the door to the garage. "Whatever happens after this, know that you have done an incredible job. I'm sure she'll talk to you about it. Have a great day!" And with that, he exited the mudroom into the garage.

I had already begun sorting through the serving pieces, separating them into trays and platters, bowls and chip/dip dishes, and then further by color and occasion, when Miffy walked in still in her bathrobe and slippers. I wasn't sure she'd even noticed me when she first came into the room until she spoke.

"Would you like a cup of coffee?" she said to me only half paying attention as she made one for herself.

"Sure. As long as you are already making one. I'd love a cup."

"Did Jack tell you?"

"Tell me what?"

"That he wants to move. That this house is too big for us."

"Oh, I guess that's what he was alluding to. Well, at least while you're here, you can use the kitchen," shrugging and smiling at her hopefully.

"He's right. In fairness, I was the one that suggested it a year ago. But that was before I got excited about staying. But he's right. Maybe one more year."

"That's plenty of time to enjoy this beautiful house... and cook in it."

"I'd like you to come back and help with downsizing and staging when the time comes."

"Absolutely. It would be my pleasure. In the meantime, I'm going to assume you will be hosting lots of parties and meals until then. So I'm going to set you up so you can entertain with ease."

"Thank you, Bonnie. You are such a joy to work with. If you don't mind, I'm going to go back to bed. Charity fundraiser last night. I had one too many. Your coffee is on the counter." She spoke over her shoulder as she walked up the back stairs to her room.

I took this moment to sit out on the back veranda

with my coffee and dream about being able to buy this manse when they put it on the market.

* * *

1. **Separate the serving pieces into trays, platters, bowls, chip/dip dishes, or any other category you own.** Easy enough.

2. **Another chance to downsize.** What is damaged, what's in poor condition, what is no longer of use to you, what do you have too many of? You get it.

3. **Sort by occasion or color.** Now, here is where it gets a little OCDish and the best way to illustrate my point is to outline what I did for Miffy & Jack.

   → All crystal and formal silver pieces were put in the dining room for the time being. I was planning to work them into the china cabinet there and any that didn't fit would be reassigned to the butler's pantry.

   → All holiday-specific pieces were brought down to the basement where I instructed Miffy and Jack to store them into the appropriately labeled boxes for that holiday.

   → What remained I organized by color, nesting

them together, and placing the stacks on each cabinet's highest shelf. Easy to see, but out of the way on a day-to-day basis. Always remember to wipe out areas with soap and water as you go.

NOTE: What to do with paper supplies? The paper party supplies were really too random to have enough of any one theme to host a party with. I suggested they eat off them until they were gone. Paper napkins and plates of various occasions from baby shower to Day of the Dead would be fun to use at any time. I placed them on the counter front and center so they would be reminded to use them.

What to do with party utensils? Plastic cake cutters, plastic serving spoons, plastic flatware, anything themed all its own drawer at the end of the counter. Also in that drawer, birthday candles and holders.

With the last big category **sorted, downsized, stacked, and stored**, the only thing left was the incidentals. And boy were there more than I first thought.

Things in this category:

→ Parchment paper, aluminum foil, plastic wrap, zipper-top bags. *I prefer a drawer especially when it comes to the bags. Open the mouth of the boxes for easy use.*
→ Cleaning supplies. *Sorted, all in one bucket,*

under the sink; like in the bathroom in Chapter 1.
- → Emergency candles, votives, and flashlights. *Somewhere you can find them when the lights go out. Matches or lighters, and batteries too should go in that space.*
- → Skewers, toothpicks, cocktail umbrellas. *Best bagged and put with the barware in the butler's pantry.*
- → Household tools. *If you don't have a small tool box, any small box will do. This is just for the quick handy essentials. Pliers, hammer, screwdrivers—flat head and Phillips.*
- → Ant traps, pens, paper. *I put ant traps with tools. Pens and paper for shopping lists somewhere near your food, either by the refrigerator or pantry.*

* * *

When I was finished, everything was neatly stored away in a cabinet or drawer, easily accessible for the task generally performed in that area. I was very happy with the results. Now to give some instructions on keeping it that way.

CLEANING & MAINTENANCE

While Miffy and Jack had a cleaning lady who washed their kitchen as if it was actually being used, you may not have that luxury. If you are handling the cleaning on your own, this is one of those "keep it neat/clean it regularly so it doesn't get out of hand" situations.

DAILY
- **Do the dishes. Wash & dry and/or fill & empty the dishwasher.** Even in a spotless kitchen, a sink full of dirty dishes makes it look unkempt. At least put them in the dishwasher until it fills for a full load. And then, after the sink is dish-free, take some dish soap and your sponge or dish rag and wash the sink down. This way, it's always clean.

NOTE: Let's talk about undermount vs. drop-in sinks with regard to cleaning. I personally prefer undermount for the very reason that you can wipe anything from the counter directly into the sink without it getting caught under the rim. If you have a drop-in sink, *as I currently do in my new house but hope to replace in a few years,* be sure to clean that edge with a pot scraper or a toothpick, something that will get into that tiny area where SO MUCH gets stuck. Now there are folks who don't like the undermount sink because they believe crud gets stuck in the area where the counter meets the sink. I say, that's far easier to keep clean because it's actually in the sink. Each time you do dishes, wash that area free of debris.

- **Wipe down the counters.** I have a personal "ick trigger" about crumbs. *Ask my daughter, she'll tell you how freaky I get about hard little crunchies on the counters.* You don't care, you say? If you want to keep your newly organized kitchen neat and tidy, you really should keep your countertops dust, stickiness, and yes, crumb free. A quick wipe down each time you make food. It's that easy.

- **Keep counters clear.** Firstly because these are food surfaces not meant for stacks of mail or dead houseplants. Secondly because you're reading this book in an attempt to get some organizing tips and that means clean and clutter free. So, if it's not food related, put it somewhere else.

WEEKLY

- **Wash major and small appliances.** Keep it clean as you use them; *no one wants to pull the door handle of the refrigerator and come away with slimy jelly fingers.* But for a serious cleaning where you take the grills and burners off the stovetop, do that once a week to keep it not only clean but in top working order. Clean anything that gets used regularly like the collection tray inside the toaster oven and the coffee maker spout.

- **Sweep and wash the floor. Wash or vacuum floor mats.** Gravity is a pain in the ass when it comes to keeping things tidy and sanitary. Depending on the number of people and pets in your house, you may need to clean your kitchen floors more than once a week. But shoot for at least once a week. It needs it more than you think. *I love a steam cleaner or wet vac for this purpose. Makes the process easier so it's not a production with a mop and pail.*

AS NEEDED
- **Wash off the containers of drippings and crusted residue.** *I'm wondering what my cocktail sauce bottle lid looks like right now.*

- **Clean out the refrigerator, pantry, and spice drawer of expired or unused foods.** Anything unopened and still within its expiration window should be used for dinner soon or be donated to a food bank.

- **Take everything out of cabinets and drawers and off shelves and wipe down with soapy water then dry.** Grease, food particles, dust go everywhere even in the cleanest of houses. *Don't think you need to do this? Open the cabinet nearest you, remove something,* *swipe your hand across the surface. I told you! You're welcome.*

- **Wash windows, light fixtures, glass-front cabinets with glass cleaner.** *Again with the kitchen and its grease-dust relationship. I don't even fry food and it's an issue in my kitchen. My seeded-glass hanging work lights are starting to look frosted. Ick!*

- **Clean under the sink. Especially if that is where your trash can is.** *I hate this job but it must be done. I know very few people with a clean under sink cabinet and even then, it's probably because they recently handled it.*

- **Downsize unused items, from corn holders shaped like cobs to turkey fryers.** *Pare down your extra always.*

I LOVE any and all Nancy Meyers films, and not just because her romantic comedies usually feature a middle-aged woman going through some life-altering dilemma *(very on brand for me)*. The reason I love them so much is the not-so-unusual attraction to her kitchen set designs. There are entire Instagram pages devoted to her kitchens. They are the quintessential ideal of creative chef-inspired cooking and effortless entertaining. The themes that run through them all are clear, clutter-free surfaces, everything you need where you use it, all organized with ease but not overly rigid, and ALWAYS CLEAN. Yes, I know it's a movie set and no one actually lives there, but that's the beauty of her design aesthetic—it looks like it IS lived in. It seems used, homey, like you could sit down to dinner or have a bowl of cereal at any point. And you'd want to, because it's inviting. You can imagine Diane Keaton wiping down the counter of crumbs after slicing you a thick piece of bread she just baked (sharpened knife and cutting board at the ready). **And all you need to do to "get it" is pare back your stuff to only what you use, organize it to make sense for use, and keep it clean by staying on top of keeping it that way.** Then you too could have a kitchen that is rom-com movie-set ready. *A-list celebrities not included.*

DECOR JUST FOR MIFFY & JACK

With relocating and organizing and a bit of cleaning on the side, it was time to dress things up a bit. This magnificent home could pull off crystal every day of the week so I pulled a crystal vase and bowl out of the china cabinet where I had just put them a few hours earlier. The vase was for the flowers I had brought and the crystal bowl was for some apples and lemons I found in the refrigerator. I placed the flowers in the center of the island and the bowl of fruit farther down the countertop near where the cutting boards were stored (another location access situation). I draped dishtowels (stored in a drawer near the stovetop with potholders) in autumnal colors, over the handles of the wall ovens and on the towel bar near the sink.

I felt I could add a bit more without it becoming too "decorated." Miffy and Jack were big University of Maryland Terps football fans, and I had found quite a bit of plastic themed serving pieces. I thought it might be whimsical to add a little vignette at the far end of the counter out of the way. Stealing a cookbook stand that was not being used, I set a UM plate on the stand and stood it up on a UM tray next to two UM tumblers. Seasonal, eye-catching, and useful. Truthfully, I wouldn't have added anything if the kitchen were smaller but ALL that blank surface area needed a little something.

I called up to Miffy that I was finished and that if she was free, I'd like her to come down so I could walk her through it. When she walked in, a grin crossed her face. Without a word, she began opening and closing cabinets and drawers. "Where did you put…oh, here it is. What about the…ah, found it." Variations on that sentiment she uttered throughout her tour. When she got to the UM decor she pointed at them and turned to me, "I thought I left these at a tailgate years ago."

"Nope. Just with all the other things. That's not a problem now."

"Unbelievable." She was just shaking her head.

"I hope you're happy with it. Do you have any questions?" I was the slightest bit concerned she wasn't thrilled with my work. She had a great poker face. I suppose that was the lawyer in her.

"I do have a question." She turned to face me. "When can you come back? Every room in this house needs your attention."

8

Can You Ever Really Have Too Many Books?

Frank Zappa is quoted as saying, "So many books, so little time." I'm not sure he ever actually said that since he's also quoted as saying, "I think it's good that books still exist, but they make me sleepy." I can't be certain either is a direct quote. But it doesn't matter. The first is appropriate in this setting.

In our abbreviation-happy world, one of my favorites is TBR or To Be Read. My TBR pile is high but not so large that I couldn't actually read through them all in this lifetime. In fact, I regularly purchase new books and pass books on that I have still not read to my community's little library. I figure, "Why should I hold onto something I'm not using when I can get it back later if I get around to wanting it?" I keep my collection of books finely tuned to the subjects that continue to interest me and I keep them to a certain square footage in my home. I don't believe every book is worth holding onto forever, though it is clear from some of the houses I have been in, not everyone agrees with me.

I recall one particular such instance in an apartment in DC. I was called in by the contractor who was hired to make renovations for a "book loving" client. He and his team were unable to do any of the work they were hired for without first hiring me. Let your imagination wander to the number of books in this one-bedroom apartment and then double it. But we'll get to Sasha's tale in a bit. First let's talk about the process of living with books.

PRACTICALITY. I'm about to lay some hard truths on you—you don't need all those books. I don't know how many books you have in your house, but you don't need them all. Want is something altogether different *(as is the compulsion to have every book in a series or every book by a single favorite author)*. But NEED? Let's discuss:

- Owning a book suggests that you will read it many times over.
- Supporting authors *(of which I am one)* and local bookstores by buying books is one thing. Holding onto them for no reason is another.
- If you ask yourself to answer honestly, do you really have any intention of reading the books you own? Even the ones unread?

Can You Ever Really Have Too Many Books?

So I'll say it again. You don't need all your books.

EFFICIENCY. I'm going to help you both to support the book community and learn to keep your collection to a serviceable amount. Funnily enough, whenever I think about books, I think about the *Twilight Zone* episode "Time Enough At Last" where the character Henry Bemis just wants time to read. If you're not finding time to read, you may want to consider downsizing your TBR pile to those books you are likely interested in enough to find that time.

- I'm not going to tell you not to buy books—*that would be career suicide for me as a writer.* But even if you probably won't read them any time soon, choose wisely and limit your purchases to books you want to OWN.

- If you want to read a book but don't need to own it, there is always the library. And more times than not, if the book is in demand, by the time your number in the queue comes up, you may actually be ready to read it.

- Filter through the books you already own. Did you buy something that you now have no interest in reading? Did you start something that wasn't as good as you expected? Has a book you bought fallen way down in the rankings on

> your TBR tower? You know what I'm going to say. Donate, sell, gift.

I love books! Even so, I believe that if you love something, set it free. Books are magical and need to be read. I have read books from the library that I then purchased because I wanted to be able to reread them at will. As for purchasing books cold, I almost always buy with the idea that eventually, I will pass them on to someone I feel may be interested in them too.

ROUTINE. Regardless of the number of books or the rooms they occupy, there are ways to keep them neat. *Dewey Decimal experience not required.*

- Ideally, use your finite space as your marker. If it doesn't fit on a shelf with your other books, something has to go.
- Rotate regularly. Just the act of seeing them may spark the interest to move them up in the rankings. If not, consider downsizing them to a new home.
- Books are made of paper which decays over time. Dust them. Check them for mildew if they are in a damp area (do not store books in a space that is moist). Make sure you are rotating them away from a window to limit fading.

Here it is. If you're not going to downsize them,

at least take care of them. A cardboard box of books stored on the floor of a garage is a straight road to destruction of property. There I said it. And frankly, what's the point of a cardboard box of books in the garage anyway…unless it's on its way to the donation center.

DECOR. Books are decor. A coffee table book is literally decor. But I'm all for dressing up a library, study, office, or reading nook with objet d'art.

- You could keep it literary themed or book useful but you don't have to. *A human skull on a shelf with Shakespeare. Marble bookends or antique treasure boxes to hold books in place. Natural wonders and curiosities, whatever piques your interest in much the same way books do.*
- Wall art, about books or not, but I personally feel the art you choose for your book space should be creative and inspiring. *For me, areas of a home that hold books are like galleries for art—important, almost sacred.*
- Sufficient light sources for reading, comfortable seating, surfaces for setting down books and drinks, warm throws, music to read by.

I often decorate with books in the homes of my clients but also my own. And why not? As I just noted above, books are like little works of art. In my humble opinion, being ensconced by objects that bring you joy and inspire you with their creativity is the very nexus of decor.

* * *

Sasha lived in the same apartment in DC for nearly 50 years. Her building was going condo and she had recently bought her unit and the one next to it. The plan was to open the wall between them and have her sister move into the adjacent apartment. She had hired a contractor to do the work, but after five decades in the same one-bedroom apartment, you can imagine the massive accumulation of stuff. Before any work could be done, everything needed to be packed up and moved offsite.

She had retired almost 15 years earlier from her job as a proofreader for a small publishing company. No surprise that she had amassed a sizable collection of books over the years. To say her living room was a room at all was a stretch. It was more like what I imagine the backroom of a poorly managed used bookstore would look like. Piles of books. Boxes of books. Open books stacked on each other, books inside of books acting as bookmarks, shelves piled high with books going every which way. And just the slightest twinge of mildew in the air.

The contractor, who was a friend of mine, told her that the work could not start until the area was cleared and he suggested she contact me for the job. This wasn't about downsizing; not yet anyway. Step one was just about getting her things out of the way so renovations could begin. My goal, once everything was in a storage unit, was to downsize and organize it there, then move it back in already knowing where everything would go. She agreed to it all *(probably thinking I wasn't going to ask her to get rid of anything)* and my assistant Jess and I started packing her up.

* * *

My suggestion with any and all projects is always to create a work area. In the last chapter it was the island in the kitchen and in the bedroom chapter, it was the bed itself. In order to create order you must have a place to put things in order. Having a storage unit in which to work was a luxury. Not only for the space but to be free of the distractions that come with being "at home." My hope was that Sasha would feel less attached to her belongings, specifically her books, once they were in a different environment.

I had the opportunity to begin my work a full day before she met me and Jess at the storage unit. During that time we **pushed all the furniture to the back of the unit, set up a few folding tables and plastic bins for sorting, and collected all the boxes of books. We dove right in and began opening boxes. Here's a look at our sorting process:**

1. **Every book was checked over for damage.**

    a. Any whiff of mildew and it was placed in a bin marked for that purpose. *The idea was to eventually throw those away but I would need Sasha's final approval.*

    b. Rips or tears were immediately taped. *I thought perhaps there was an appropriate tape to use for this process but Sasha said she would be happy with any clear household tape.*

2. **Hardcover, paperback, and coffee table books were separated.**

    a. First sorting was just by these criteria. Further sorting would follow by subject and size.

    b. During this process all books were wiped down to remove dust and cobwebs. *Wearing some kind of face covering and surgical gloves is a must. First for the debris, second for the paper cuts.*

3. **Starting with the smallest assortment (coffee table books):**

    a. The books were sorted by subject matter (travel, architecture, art, interior design, etc.).

b. Each subject matter was then put into size order, reboxed, labeled, and set with the furniture at the back of the storage unit. *I did not feel there was a significant amount of books in the category to warrant Sasha having to downsize it. All these books could be worked into the decor in her newly expanded home.*

4. **Next onto hardcover books:**

   a. The books were separated into fiction and nonfiction, and in a few cases, foreign language *(which neither Jess nor I could determine the genre for).*

   b. We then separated each collection by subject as best we could (crime, historical, romance, feminism, Jewish studies, etc.).

   c. Finally, we placed them in clear plastic bins, spines up, for a final assessment from Sasha. *When we were finished, we had 15 bins of books. I had forewarned Sasha that hardcover books would have to be whittled down to 10 bins or fewer. (More on that later.)*

5. **Lastly, paperback books:**

   a. Same as before, the books were separated into fiction, nonfiction, and foreign language.

b. Each collection was separated into subject matter.

c. Finally, all books stacked on the table in piles, for a final pass by Sasha. *We had run out of bins sorting the hardcover books, so we left these stacked on the tables. I was hoping most of these could be donated.*

With sorting complete, Jess and I closed up shop for the day and got a well-deserved dinner. We were working at such a steady fast pace, we hadn't stopped for lunch, and it was already 7:30pm. I texted Sasha to meet us at the storage unit at 8am the next day. She grumbled about it being too early but I assured her that if she was serious about getting a beautiful new home at the end of this process, that we would be done by lunch. *Famous last words.*

* * *

Sasha showed up at 9am the next day. In the hour before, I had already gone through all the stages of anxiety, frustration, anger, and had come around to "whatever." When she entered the unit without acknowledging she had made us wait, I went right into my speech stating plainly the facts and explaining what we had done.

"Good morning, Sasha. Let me start by explaining

what we handled yesterday. First off, all books have been repaired for noticeable tears and rips. All your coffee table books have been separated and cleaned. No need to go through those. I can work all of them into the decor. Now we have your hardcover books over here. We separated them by subject as best we could. We will need to pare down about a third of the books."

"What do you mean 'pare down'?"

"You won't have sufficient room for all of them. I've seen the blueprints for the new built-in bookcases, and they won't all fit. I have a few donation centers and used bookstores in mind that would love them."

"I hired you to organize them, not get rid of them."

"Well actually, you hired us to move them, organize them, and redecorate with them in your new home but in order to have a truly new home, these are not all going to fit. Let's do it this way. Do you need all of these? There must be a few that you more than likely won't read again. Let's just start with those."

"No. I'm tired now. Find a way to make them all fit."

"Sasha, in your apartment the way it was, you had books on the floor and books behind other books. That's going to happen again if we don't sort through and take some out."

"I'm okay with that."

I fell silent. Jess looked at me with a "now what" expression. I turned back to Sasha.

"Okay. Then if you are really okay with that, then that's what we'll do. Tell me, what is your favorite subject matter so I can put that at eye level on the shelves?"

"Crime and historical fiction and nonfiction. I have a lot of romance too but I don't read those much."

"We could put those behind the other books. Or maybe we could gift them to a local library?"

"No. Just put them behind."

"Got it. One last thing. We have a box over here filled with books that may have some moisture damage because they are beginning to mildew. Can we just dispose of those?"

"No. I have a storage locker in the basement of the building. Just put them there."

"I don't mind taking care of them. I can drop them at the municipal trash place on my way home."

"No. They aren't garbage."

And with that, Sasha left. Jess and I just looked at each other and shook our heads. "Well, looks like we can head out. And we got paid for the day anyway," Jess said, collecting her bag, "Coffee's on me."

* * *

Do you love books? Do you have an inordinate amount of books? Please do yourself and your books a favor and treat them well. If Sasha had been accepting of the task, **I would have walked her through the following questions to help release at least some of her books.**

- Are they damaged by mildew? *Mildew will destroy the book and give your home a pungent odor. They should be thrown away.*

- Are they damaged with rips and tears? *Repair them. Or get rid of them. Paperback books can be recycled. Hardcover can and should be mended or donated.*

- Of the books you own, how many have you read at all? How many have you reread? Do you have any intention of reading them? Or rereading them? *There, I'm afraid, is your answer to whether or not you should keep them.*

- As I said before at the start of this chapter, did you buy something that you now have no interest in reading? Did you start something that wasn't as good as you expected? Has a book you bought fallen way down in the rankings on your TBR tower? *You know what I'm going to say. Donate, sell, gift.*

Yes, we all have them. That book you bought on vacation in that quaint bookshop with the cat sitting in the window and the kindly old man with spectacles giving you your change in pennies. Maybe you read the first chapter while standing in the stacks and you can't wait to devour more, but after vacation you're back to work with no time to read and that precious little book has been placed on the bedside table with the rest of the "to be read." Fear not! If you really want to read it, you will find time. If once you're home it doesn't hold the same allure for you, don't feel you have to hold onto it. Gift it to a friend with a note that says you'd love to read it after them. Donate it to your local little library or actual library. Sell it online for almost the cover price. Or find time to read it through and then, if you deem it worthy of a reread, keep it. Otherwise, why are you really holding onto it?

SIDE STORY: There are standard American classics read by nearly all high school students decade after decade. I held onto mine with the idea of rereading them as I got older; *"Catcher in the Rye" lands a whole lot differently at 50 than it did at 15.* The bonus of holding onto them was that when my daughter read them, she used mine—*BORROMEO written in marker along the page edge, TOMLINSON added to it after.* Now, that classic has a family history.

I'm never going to tell you to get rid of things that have purpose and meaning. EVER! I'm only trying to hint that not everything you own is worth keeping if you ask yourself the right questions.

* * *

Three weeks later, the work was complete in Sasha's new double-sized condo. She had a cleaning crew come through and now it was move-in day. My focus was to get all the furniture in and placed before working on the books. She had contracted for six floor-to-ceiling bookcases built along the living room walls. I knew it still would not be enough but I was determined to make it look lovely regardless.

During construction, Sasha had been staying with her sister in Alexandria, VA, and planned to stay through the move-in as well. That was a huge help to me and Jess. We could forge on with our plans without interruption and make adjustments after Sasha arrived.

1. We stacked all the romance paperback books along the back of each lower shelf on every bookcase. *This actually proved to be beneficial at preventing books on the lower shelves from getting pushed back out of sight.*

2. As requested, crime and historical books, both fiction and nonfiction, were lined on the shelves at eye level. We did not delve further into organizing by author, instead choosing to go with a more aesthetically pleasing look of organizing by size. Hardcover books lined up; paperback books stacked for decor interest, sometimes across, sometimes in stacks. *By*

> *stacking some books and lining up others, you can essentially use the stacked books as bookends. But honestly, it's more about how boring I think a row of book spines look on a home library shelf. Mix it up! Maybe even display a front-facing book as your pick-of-the-week.*

3. Each subject was slotted in using the same method.

4. Coffee table books were laid on the coffee table in three stacks of two to three books depending on size. The remaining were stacked on various end tables and surfaces throughout the living room and primary bedroom.

When all was complete, we had one bin of books left. Jess had the great idea of separating out one subject and moving it into her sister's new bedroom. We opted to put "travel" there and it gave us the space we needed in the living room to make the adjustments. Surrounded by empty boxes and thoroughly exhausted, we called it a day and decided to meet back there in the morning.

I spoke with Sasha that night to outline what had been done and what we planned to accomplish next. That's when she told me that her sister would have no room for the books we placed there.

"Okay. No worries. We'll take care of it. I'll touch

base with you later tomorrow. Thank you, Sasha." I ended the call and went right to bed. *Sleep from exhaustion came fast.*

* * *

The next morning, Jess and I met outside the building and sat on a park bench to have breakfast. "I hate to say it, but I'm losing steam for this project," I said, taking a long drink from my coffee.

"I lost it when she said 'no' to throwing out the mildewed books," Jess replied with a wide-eyed look.

"Let's talk game plan. We've placed the living room furniture and handled the organization and decor of the books. So, we are basically finished. We just have to pull the books from the other bedroom, do final touches in the living room, check the storage unit in the basement to see how the movers left things, and then we're done."

"We have to sweep out the unit, check that nothing was left behind," Jess reminded me.

"Right, right. Okay, good. Where do you think we should put those travel books?" I said to Jess as I finished the last of my coffee.

"What about in the bathroom? I know how you feel about books in the bathroom but we are out of space."

"Ugh! Well, even if I agreed, there is so little room there anyway. You know what? Let's just stack them under the side tables. Just for decor purposes."

"Sounds like a plan."

CLEANING & MAINTENANCE

Not much in the cleaning category when it comes to books but dusting *(and if I had my way, downsizing)*.

- **Feather dusting is fine with added focus on the spine.**
- **Repair as needed.**
- **Downsize regularly.**
- **And the slightest off-putting scent should suggest you put it out with the trash.**

DECOR JUST FOR SASHA

I said earlier in the chapter how I feel about books. They are to me, little treasure boxes—interesting curiosities, inspiring creativity, whisking the reader off on flights of fancy. And so too, I believe, should the objects and trinkets that you use as decor with them. Sasha had plenty to work with in her collections so it was more a matter of editing than finding things to use.

- Jess was handling the **artwork** throughout and I left all the decision-making with regard to that to her. She had an eye for art, the talent for spatial-relations in a room, and the skill to hang them properly. *She was a gift of an assistant.*

- Sasha had two sets of **marble bookends** but with so many actual books taking up the shelves and no need to keep them in place, we used the bookends as decor on top of the coffee table books.

- There were several baseball-sized **geodes** which I placed on the stacks of books on the bottom shelves. *Bottom shelves don't get the attention they deserve so I like to dress them up a bit.*

- Sasha had many **framed photos.** Some from her travels to Asia and Israel, others with her family and friends. I tried to tuck them in on the shelves with common themes, also adding a collection of frames in her bedroom. *Of course, adding anything to a bookshelf that requires it be taken down to remove a book is not ideal. But I made an executive decision and went with it.*

When we were finished, we stepped back to look at the work. We had done A LOT! But one more thing had to be done. We had to test it out. We each went to the shelf and chose a book.

- Was it easy to pull from the shelf?
- Did things fall over when it was removed?
- Was there a comfy place to sit nearby? With enough light as well?

- Did it feel like a home and not a cold library or a staged bookstore?

It passed all our tests and we were ready for the last one. I called Sasha who was having lunch with her sister around the corner. Some 30 minutes later they entered the newly organized and decorated living room. Sasha's sister Anya spoke first.

"You had all these beautiful new shelves built but you kept all the crappy books?"

Jess elbowed me in the side and I stifled a laugh.

"Hey! It's my house. I can do what I want. You've got your own living space," Sasha shot back.

"Thank God!" Anya said. Then she turned to me with a smile and a sweet tone while also grabbing Jess's arm. "Dear, it looks beautiful. It can't have been easy to find space for all her books. You did a great job. You'll have to come back and do my place up next."

"We would love to. Thank you." And with that she gently touched the side of Jess's face in a grandmotherly way, turned to Sasha and said, gesturing to me, "Tip her well."

"Big sister over here, still telling me what to do. Okay Bonnie so let's talk about this. It's very nice. But I don't see all my books here and I was very clear that I didn't want to get rid of any."

"Not to worry. They are all present and accounted

for with the exception of the books that we stored in your storage area in the basement. The romance paperbacks are stacked behind the books on the bottom shelves. You had said they were not of particular interest to you but you didn't want to part with them so we found a way to handle that."

"Oh. Yes. Then it all looks very nice. Thank you. I'm very happy with the work you two have done. And I would love to have you back to do the rest. Maybe in a few weeks."

I looked at Jess whose eyes got ever-so-slightly wider. Then I replied to Sasha, "We would love to, but unfortunately we have a full calendar for the next two months. Can I call you next week with some dates?"

"Of course, dear," she said, handing me a check for the balance of our work. "I look forward to it."

"As do I Sasha, it was a pleasure. And so nice to meet you, Anya. We'll see you both again soon."

* * *

Jess and I walked out of the building and into the midafternoon sun, tired, dirty, and just a bit relieved that she was happy.

9

Look at That! I Can See the Floor!

It always surprises me how many people use their garage for storage instead of for vehicles. What is in those boxes and bins that is worth keeping securely indoors while vehicles, costing tens of thousands of dollars, sit outside through seasons of sun, sap, and snow. Maybe you just couldn't figure out how to make it all work—a garage serving as both storage AND vehicular home. Or maybe you never intended it to be more than a storage unit. Whatever your goal, this important and incredibly useful space needs your attention and care. *So maybe don't just throw things into it from the doorway.*

PRACTICALITY. Practicality is your garage's only purpose. Of course, in recent years, garages have become man-caves and she-spaces, but that is not their intended purpose. Their reason for being is to provide security and cover for your:

- Vehicle (one or more)
- Outdoor lawn/garden equipment if you do not have a shed
- Tools, both general household and specific to your needs and interests
- Outdoor sports/leisure items (balls, camping equipment, etc.)
- Trash and recycling bins

So you can see why it would make me just the slightest bit irritated to find that people deposit items like high school yearbooks and holiday table linens packed in cardboard boxes in the garage. One, they don't belong there. Two, the mice will graciously accept your invitation for them to move in. (Substitute mice for whatever wildlife resides in your area.)

EFFICIENCY. Take any slapstick comedy and watch the main character drive into their too-tight garage, not be able to open the car door, and shimmy out the sunroof. Or they can get the door open but in doing so, hit the wall, the shelves come down, and they are bombarded by balls and an open can of paint. It's funny because it's an exaggeration of reality, one that home organizers see more times than they'd like to

Look at That! I Can See the Floor!

admit. But there are ways to plan out your garage so you have the appropriate space.

- First and foremost, don't fill it up! Downsize your belongings. *Do you really need three hatchets when you have split wood delivered? Did you ever need three?*

- Use the walls and ceiling to get things up off the floor. Not only does this provide more space but if you do park your vehicle in the garage, you will bring in rain and snow which will make the floor wet, and as a result anything sitting on the floor wet. *Always, always, attach shelves, hooks, etc., to studs or rafters. This is a working room. It requires serious heavy-duty accessories.*

- Utilize creative storage solutions, bought or makeshift, so that things stay where you put them. *I'm going to give you one of my favorite on-the-fly hacks—I definitely had my coffee that morning. Using a ping-pong table net nailed across the front of a shelf can prevent balls from falling off while still providing easy access.*

- Leave space around your vehicle so that doors can swing open, even if not fully wide. *For me, that space must consider me and any of my huge handbags. I like a big bag! Some of you are with me there.*

A working space has to work. If it does not, you must make adjustments or the space will lose sight of its purpose.

ROUTINE. Keep it neat, consistently. Enough said.

- If you take it out, put it back where it belongs, not just back in the garage in any old place.
- If you begin to accumulate beyond your needs, downsize. Do it anyway, annually.
- Sweep out monthly, clean out annually. Keep an eye out for signs of critters. *I have always lived in wooded areas. As a result, my garage has nearly always hosted some wildlife. From mice to snakes, spiders to hornets. My daughter once stepped out into the garage and nearly tripped over a turtle. If you don't see them, it doesn't mean they aren't there.*

I'm going to say this once and then I'll stop. Your garage is not a catchall for the crap you "downsized" from the rest of the house. And it is not a dump for what you don't use anymore. Nor is it a throwaway space just because it's not inside your house. Treat everything in your world with respect! *Rant over. I do apologize for being blunt. I just feel very strongly about this forgotten child of the house.*

DECOR. Some of you are going to disagree with me here but this is a book about organizing—don't decorate your garage. *You don't need a neon Coors Light sign or twinkle lights.* The decor should come from the neat, efficient, user-friendly nature of the space. But if you must, I suppose you could keep it useful.

- Sufficient overhead light. *The light on the garage door opener is not enough.*
- Shelves, storage bins, hanging bike racks. *Always based on your needs.*
- Garage floor containment mats, *to contain anything dripping off or from the car.*

Let's be practical and logical here. If you can't get your vehicle in the garage because there is too much stuff, adding decor will not help.

* * *

I have never before, nor since, worked in a garage quite like the one owned by my client Matt. Matt considered himself a DIYer. He was really more of a collector of tools; tools he opened, used once and then not again. He was also a collector of projects—broken electronics to fix, old furniture to refinish, and garage sale finds he could "make into something." But with all the projects cluttering the garage, he didn't have space to work in, which is why he called me.

On the day scheduled, he asked me to meet him at the garage. As I pulled into the driveway, the garage door opened as if on cue. It was quite the reveal especially when a tower of cardboard boxes began to waver as the base of the door rose past them. I hadn't yet seen Matt as I got out of the car but I heard him, rummaging around like a large animal foraging in the woods.

"Matt? Are you in there?" I called out from the driveway.

"Yeah. Give me a second. It's really messy in here. I'll be right out." When he rose from the rubble of his disaster-of-a-garage, he waved for me to come closer. "All set, come and take a look."

I inched my way closer to the garage, being careful to avoid the sharp tools pointing up out of a bucket at the only entrance through the chaos. *"How do I get out of doing this project?" I thought to myself.*

"So here it is," Matt said with a flourish of his arms.

"Yes indeedy," I replied, eyes wide in sarcastic fear, *coupled with a bit of actual fear. This looked like somewhere you'd find a decomposing body.* "So Matt, what is it you are hoping I can do for you?"

"Make some sense out of this hellhole. It's gotten beyond my control."

"Be honest, Matt," I said jokingly, head tilted, grin on my face. "Did you ever really have control in here?"

"Well, okay. It was better. Not up to your standards, I'm sure, but better."

"Okay, no worries. I'd like to take some photos while we chat if you don't mind."

"Be my guest," he said, moving out of the way so I could step past him.

"Tell me, how do you want to use this space? Do you want it to be all workshop? You didn't want a car in here, did you?"

"No. No car. But my yard tools are in here too. Lawn mower, shovel, that kind of thing."

"There's a lawn mower in here?"

"Yeah, right in the corner." Matt pointed to the far back corner of the garage. The gas-powered push mower was on top of a stack of wood.

"A-ha. Well I'm sure I can find better access to the outside so you don't have to maneuver over and around so many things to use it."

"Yeah, that's probably a good idea."

Dear Lord, this place was a disaster. I was afraid of being cut on something if I ventured too much farther in, so I took the remainder of the photos from the driveway. I had Matt use my measuring tape for some quick measurements inside the space, then we discussed the timeline and I said I'd get back to him in a few days with a proposal.

"While you work up your plans, I was thinking of

three stations so I can do multiple projects at the same time. I like to bounce between projects when I get bored with one of them."

"Surprisingly enough, you have the space for it. It will just depend on what we have to work with. What I'd like you to consider in the meantime, is what you can get rid of, either at the dump or by selling or donating. Would you mind going through it over the next week?"

"Ah, I need all the tools and machines."

"Okay, but just for fun, give it a once-over. You may be surprised by what you find. Give me a few days to get back to you with my proposal."

"Thanks for your help, I really appreciate it."

"Not at all, Matt. It's my job and my pleasure. I'll get in touch as soon as possible. We can begin work in a few weeks if you accept the bid."

"That would be fantastic."

I got back in my car, having barely entered the garage, but still somehow feeling like I was covered in dirt and sawdust. This was going to be a physically grueling project, but I held out hope that Matt would be happy with the work AND able to keep it organized once the work was completed.

* * *

So you want to clean out your garage and make it a usable space in your home? I'm going to be honest up front. This is a big project. It takes planning, effort, focus, and a good chunk of time. But once it's complete, your only regret will be not doing it sooner. It is so satisfying!

Depending on how much is in your garage, this process could easily take several days to a week. Plan your work around the weather, ideally a block of straight sunny days. Have tarps on hand to cover any items in the driveway when you are done for the day. **Let's break this down:**

1. **Pull everything out of the garage.** The joy of working in this space is the ability to pull everything out into the driveway. Leave nothing behind unless it's attached in some way and even then, adjustments may still be made.

2. **Sweep out the garage. Wash the floor if necessary.** All sorts of things collect on the floor of a garage. If it doesn't sweep away, wash it away. *Bear in mind, this is just so you have a clean place to work. You will have to do it again at the end.*

3. **Clear out any critters.** With a flashlight and a broom, sweep down the walls and inside any nooks and crannies. Same for shelving or rafters that are already in place. Take this time to thoroughly clean out cobwebs and treat for

bugs or rodents if that is an issue. *You may not mind having a few furry visitors, but they can make a disaster of your belongings. Believe me, no one wants to open their camping equipment come spring to find a family of mice.*

4. **Assess organizing needs. Do not accessorize for what you do not have.** If you don't have bikes, you don't need a bike rack, even if it looks cool hanging from your ceiling. Yes, you could go all out outfitting your space like an advertisement for GarageTek but that's not going to keep you neat. Especially if you install organizers that don't address your storage needs. **Make a detailed shopping list.** *My advice is to order everything you need online from a big box store and schedule it for curbside pickup. This way you won't waste time or money walking through the store.*

NOTE: When it comes to outfitting your garage, determine first if you possibly have something on hand to do the job without purchasing something new. **That's my "make do" principle.** That ping-pong net trick from before is one that I love and have used on several jobs.

5. **Consider lighting or exhaust fans if needed.** You could do this work yourself by stringing

extension cords across the ceiling or you could call in a professional. Either way, make it as neat as possible by tying up extra cord with a zip tie or elastic.

6. **Install organizers either built-in or stand-alone.** This is the time to build shelves or install heavy-duty hooks—I prefer the ones that are vinyl coated so whatever you hang not only grips in place but will not scratch. Consider a large tool chest on wheels or a plastic chest with doors for storing things like pool accessories. Whether you purchased these organizers or created them with some out-of-the-box thinking, as long as you NEED it, now is the time to put it in place.

7. **Head out to the driveway and start sorting by category. Downsize as you go.** Tools, paint, automotive, whatever you pulled out of your garage, sort it based on use. Don't attempt to do more than just that for this step. *If you discover items in your garage that are not garage specific, address the issue accordingly and as soon as possible. See story.*

SIDE STORY: I have a friend who was storing several large boxes of unknown items in her garage for friends of hers and she really wanted the room for another car.

"I don't have room in my garage for my daughter's car. These boxes take up a lot of space."

"What's in them?"

"I'm not sure."

"How long have you had them?"

"Years."

"That's too long to ask a friend to store stuff for you. I think they all must have forgotten about them. Why don't you give them each a call and ask what they'd like to do with them?"

Long story short, all boxes were gone in a few days. One friend had indeed forgotten about them and picked them up. Another friend had also forgotten but didn't want them anymore so my friend dropped them off at a donation center. Problem solved as soon as she addressed the issue head on. Sometimes it's that easy. Don't put it off. Do!

8. **Prep garbage can and recycling bins.** Use construction grade trash bags so they won't break. Have a few cardboard boxes, perhaps the ones you just emptied as you sorted, for donations.

9. **Take any one category and sort further.** Matt had loads of circuit boards and soldering tools. I rummaged through his other items to find a plastic lidded tote large enough to hold it all and a smaller one to fit inside. Then I:

a. Wiped each piece down with a dry rag.

b. Bound electrical cords with rubber bands.

c. Lined up all the boards on their long end in size order.

d. Added the tools and materials to a smaller bin and placed it inside.

e. Labeled the bin on the outside with a Sharpie marker, *since it was opaque and not clear.*

f. Placed it back in the garage in a temporary, but possibly permanent, location.

10. **Address each category in turn, placing each back in the garage when finished.** During this step, you may find that the plan in your head isn't quite working. That's okay. Nothing is set in stone. Not even the brackets you attached to the wall studs. Adjust accordingly. Not just for spatial purposes but for efficiency purposes. Say for example your tools are across the garage from the door into the house and you find that you regularly need a screwdriver. Either keep a small set of tools in the house or move the tools from the far side of the garage to a space near the door. *"What a very specific suggestion, Bonnie," you say. To which I would*

> *reply, "Well, have you ever crossed your garage to get a tool on the other side wearing only socks and stepped in a pool of water that ran off your car from driving in the rain? I have. Move the tools."*

SIDE STORY: If you should ever be in the market to hire a professional organizer, the rates and terms vary wildly. Ask up front how they determine their cost. Some work hourly and the rates are anywhere from $50-$200 an hour. That adds up over the course of a few days.

My process was always to meet with the client first, photograph and measure the space, and most importantly discuss what the client's expectations were for the end result. It was then that I would adjust those expectations accordingly, usually based on the amount of stuff versus space and the very real need to downsize said stuff. Also considered in the cost:

- need to bring in my assistant Jess
- need to hire a handyman to install fixtures or movers to handle large pieces of furniture
- estimate of the number of days and hours each day needed
- estimate of physical exertion required *(not all jobs are equal)*
- estimate, in some cases, of the anxiety working with a difficult client or an exceptionally

> soiled space *(think celebrity closet versus hoarder house)*

Sometimes, my rates seem higher than expected to the client and that's when I offer the option to do the work themselves using notes I will custom make for them *at a much lower rate.* Once they see what goes into the project, they realize it's worth paying me to do it after all. I've never had a client complain about the cost once they've seen the final result. And even after all the planning that goes into a proposal, I somehow always seemed to underbid what it actually took to do the work so the client always won in the end anyway.

* * *

Matt was looking to turn a two-car garage into three distinct work areas for his menagerie of interests and equipment. Currently the garage was dangerously haphazard with no order and no actual footpath other than the one that required walking on discarded tools and trash. He admitted to me that his ADHD was as much to blame as his lack of motivation but he never had a system so he was hoping this would be something he could maintain. He accepted my proposal and work began a few weeks later. During that time, I had the opportunity to study the photos I took and determine what, if any, storage supplies I should bring. But with so much in the space, I could no more determine what he needed than if he already had the materials I could use to cobble something together. I decided to bring a few extra-large heavy-duty bins and extra-large iron hooks with me because, if nothing else, he needed those.

Following the basic outline above, Jess and I began pulling everything out of the garage, but we also attempted to separate the contents in the driveway into categories to get a jumpstart on that task. You can do the same as long as it doesn't slow down your momentum. If it's all just a mixed bag of randomness, moving everything out to clear the garage is a much faster way to go. You can separate in step 7.

Once we had everything out of the garage and somewhat separated into categories in the driveway, Jess took up the task of sweeping and critter removal *(and boy did I thank her for it because she found more than a few—I'll leave it at that)*. While she handled the cleanup, I was contemplating the best ways to provide the necessary storage and floor plans based on both what Matt had to work with and what he wanted overall. He had a few built-in shelves but he needed more. Many more. Thankfully, he had the boards and brackets on hand since it had been his goal to add more, and with my trusty electric drill I started hanging the shelves.

NOTE: Always work with work gloves, protective eyewear, and a KN95 face mask in unfinished basements, attics, and garages. *If you've ever blown your nose after a project in one of these spaces, the crud in the tissue is just what didn't get into your lungs. And the first time the palm of your hand scrapes across a nail, you'll remember I said this.*

Shelves hung, floor swept, critters gone, and items separated in the driveway, it was time to set up the three individual work stations. If this had been a typical garage project, we would have determined the best storage options around the perimeter of the garage allowing enough room for vehicles. But here, cars were not the priority, working on projects with tools and materials was. We had to consider not just the storage, but an unobstructed area to move within.

Given his varied interests and lack of organization, it was important that I structure the room to meet not only the way he worked but the flow into and out of the garage to both the driveway and the house. I was also plagued with an escape plan in the event of emergencies. *I had this recurring vision of an electrical fire and he couldn't get out because the exits were blocked.* As a result, I purchased three surprise gifts.

With all this in mind, I decided to start at the beginning with this question: what were each of these stations going to be for? Surveying the piles of items we had removed from the garage, two categories were strong contenders—wooden furniture repair and electronics. A third was not yet presenting itself. I took it on faith that it would present itself as we worked.

I decided that the furniture repair station would be set farthest from the door that led into the house. Why? Because it created the most debris thus the greatest chance for tracking said debris indoors. Setting it farthest away might offer a bit less mess in the house. Jess and I moved one of the extremely heavy wooden work tables into place leaving enough room to move around it comfortably to work as well as retrieve things from the wall shelves behind it. With a clear focus for the purpose of this station, we began to fill the section with the appropriate tools and materials. Tools were in clear plastic bins set on the wall shelves, while larger ones were hung on hooks. Large standing equipment was rolled into place in easy proximity to wall outlets with their cords taped down to the floor. A box of tiny drawers with screws and nails was sorted and set on the tabletop for easy access. Wood planks were stacked across the back wall on cinder blocks so the wood would not come in contact with the sometimes wet or moist floor, and smaller pieces of wood were placed in bins and slid under the worktable for easy access. I also stored the shop vac there to encourage its use during and after all work in this area. Lastly, I secured one of my gifts, a small fire extinguisher, to a back leg of the table in case of emergency. There was more to be done to finish off this section but we wanted to create

Look at That! I Can See the Floor!

the broad strokes so we moved onto what would be the center work area of the garage—electronics.

The next table was set in place again providing comfortable space around all four sides. Two large tool boxes with the contents sorted and arranged were placed on top of the table providing easy access to all essential needs. A lighted magnifying glass with extension arm was secured to the table top for working with intricate equipment and a stool for these same projects was placed beneath the bench next to that bin with circuit boards I discussed earlier. Lastly, another fire extinguisher was added *(that recurring vision was no joke)*.

We positioned the last table in the available space and Jess and I stepped out into the driveway to get a big picture look at what we were creating. This third work area still did not have a clear focus. Everything that was left fell into the category of potential projects or "things that could be turned into something else."

"What do you think of this?" I said to Jess in mild exhaustion while we both stood facing the garage. "What if we move the electronics station closest to the entrance into the house, then slot the empty table in the center of the room to use for storage for the rest of the stuff. We can separate all these leftovers as best we can into some semblance of categories and bin them, then put them below and on top of the table. They will be neat and labeled so he can find what he wants but we don't dedicate the space for work as much as storage. He can always clear it to use if he needs it. It's not ideal but I'm running out of steam here."

"That'll work, but how about this twist?" Jess began, using the space between her hands as measurement to test her theory. "What if we move electronics to the area closest to the house like you said, but we double up the wood station which could probably use more surface area anyway, leaving a little gap between the two tables, just enough for him to work around. We can still separate and bin the leftovers but we store them across the back wall instead. What do you think?"

"Yes! Thank you! That's the plan! I say we call it a night and get a fresh start in the morning."

* * *

When all was said and done, we had created a workable space for Matt. One where he had room to move freely and one where he was able to find everything he needed easily. We had considered space for specific work and the storage to keep what he needed within a few steps of that work area. We needed very little for this project but to give the garage order and purpose. Sorting and cleaning seemed to be our biggest tasks. I did suggest that there were a few unmarked bottles of solvent or adhesive or who-knows-what that he should consider disposing of properly as they could pose a hazard; at the very least label them and put them with the work area to which they belong. We walked him through the space, showed him where everything was and why, and told him about the new fire extinguishers attached to each table as a precaution. I also asked that he consider downsizing some of his supplies.

"Matt, we have separated these materials as best we could. I'd like you to think about getting rid of some. I'd like to say half but 25% is good too. I can see by the condition they are in that you have not touched them in some time and, honestly, you may not. That's not judgment, it's just what I see as the reality of the situation. You prefer the two hobbies we have made a priority. If you were to get rid of a quarter of these things that you are not using, you would have that much more space to work without clutter. More importantly, you'd have the mental headspace to be more creative." I paused waiting for Matt to take in what I said. He had grown very silent and was looking forlornly at the bins amassed across the back wall.

"I'll think about it, for sure. But I'm going to work with it the way it is and maybe I won't have to."

"That makes sense. Good. Well then, we're all done here. Oh, wait! One last thing… "

CLEANING & MAINTENANCE

"I made you a little utility cubby. It's got a couple brooms and dustpans, a bucket with scrub brushes and some liquid soap. And I've already shown you where the shop vac is stored. What I suggest is once a week you sweep or vacuum the floors and vacuum the worktables. Empty the contents immediately after so it doesn't build up in the vacuum. I've set up your recycling and trash bins right outside the garage to the left of the door. You previously had them just in the driveway but this way, if you do purchase more furniture to work on, you can pull your truck right up to the door without hitting any of the cans. As for your lawnmower, ideally I would like to see it stored in a shed or a large outdoor storage box. I know Rubbermaid makes one with doors so you could roll it right in and lock it securely. In the meantime, I have it hiding under the second woodworking table but that's really just for now."

"Got it! I've been looking at one of those storage boxes. I'll get it this week. And yes, I think I can keep up with the cleaning. I want to, it's just a matter of doing it."

"I know you can do it! I have faith in you. I also know that now that it's organized here, you will be able to work better. I think the clutter may have been stunting your creativity."

"It absolutely was. Thank you. It looks amazing in here. I'm not really sure how you pulled it off."

"Teamwork, and the single-minded focus to give you a proper work space. Now remember, you and I set up an appointment for next month. I'll come back out and make adjustments if something doesn't feel right. But I think you've got a good place to start from."

"I would agree. Let me grab my checkbook. You need to be paid."

DECOR JUST FOR MATT

Maybe I'd consider a white board so he could write down ideas and prioritize projects but only if he downsized by half because there was no visible wall space to hang one. Otherwise, no decor; it's a garage.

10

Where Did I Put That Thing?

Earlier this year, I lost my daughter's passport and she wound up having to go through the process of getting a replacement. Thankfully she wasn't heading out of the country when we discovered it was missing, but it was my fault. She gave it to me to put back in the safe and I thought I had. But when I went to retrieve it, it wasn't there. We searched EVERYWHERE, tearing the house and my car apart for three days. Suffice it to say, I thought I was losing my mind when I couldn't place at all where I had put it.

Eventually, her now defunct passport was found. Apparently, when I was moving her out of her dorm for the summer, I had slipped it into the pocket of a bag—a bag that belonged to a friend of hers who had asked to store it at our house over the summer. At the start of the new semester, once the bag was returned to her friend, the friend found it and returned it to her, and that's when I remembered what happened—my daughter had handed me her passport but my handbag was on the floor of the passenger seat, and since I didn't want this very important document to be loose in the car, I put it in the nearest pocket for safekeeping. Of course, once home, I forgot to remove it and put it in its rightful place. Case closed. *Though I hate to tell you, reader, that my daughter's campus is less than half an hour away from the house, so forgetting about it completely in that time is not only utterly embarrassing but also possibly cause for an appointment with a neurologist.*

* * *

We're at the last chapter of the book. I hope you've found some useful tools, possibly a new way to approach things, maybe even just some motivation. We all get disorganized, myself included. But if you're reading this book, you were searching for a bit of help and I hope you found it in these pages. This last chapter is not room specific. It's about creating muscle memory for where things go and, in the process, save your sanity, budget, and time. Life is too short and time is too precious to waste any of it searching for stuff you misplaced. *Those three days I lost looking for a passport are days I will never get back. I don't want that for you.*

PRACTICALITY. Why is being organized worth the effort to set in motion?

- It looks neat and tidy but, more importantly, various studies have been done on the importance of keeping your habitat clean, orderly, and clutter free. Disorganization can be psychologically damaging and can wreak havoc on your motivation, inspiration, and thought processes.
- Finding what you need every time you need it frees up time better spent on living your best life.
- Monetarily, you will save by not having to replace lost items. *A replacement passport is $130, by the way.*

Being organized comes naturally to me. I understand that is not everyone's MO. But I can't stress enough that adding some order to your surroundings will improve your life, not just from the ease of locating things but from removing the mental block that disorder has on your thinking and mood.

EFFICIENCY. It's not just about putting things away so you don't see it. It's about putting them somewhere that makes sense for how you use them.

- If you store it where you use it, you save time in retrieving it.
- If you store it where you use it, you don't halt the task at hand or slow your momentum to retrieve it.
- If you store it where you use it, in an accessible place to meet the needs of the task at hand, the rhythm created is like a dance.

Think of a chef in a Michelin star restaurant and the seamless orchestration of a perfectly attuned kitchen and staff. Tools at the ready, stations for each component of a dish, guidelines that create precision, not waste of time or resources. Those same principles can be applied in your home and with far less effort than you think.

ROUTINE. It's not just about getting organized so that it looks good for the "after shot". It's about building a space that basically keeps itself in order.

- But you do need to maintain it. A little every day or at least as often as you use it.
- If you find that it's difficult to maintain, being organized isn't the problem, it's how it's been organized. Feel free to adjust so that the process takes less effort. Less maintenance is always the goal.

- If you have something, keep it neat. First for appearance, second for ease of use, third out of respect for your belongings, your surroundings, and yourself.

Maintaining your organized space is an ongoing process but one that should be somewhat effortless once you get in the habit where muscle memory takes over. You naturally know that milk goes in the refrigerator. You wouldn't put it anywhere else in your home. When you need milk, you don't stop and think "where did I put it?" In fact, you don't think at all. Your body naturally moves to the refrigerator and probably even knows where to reach for it without looking. Now, think of that on a larger scale in all areas of your life. Think of the time saved.

DECOR. There is little to discuss in this chapter with regard to decor. Dress your home for your tastes and budget. I will suggest when considering decor through an organizer's lens you examine the following.

- How much do you want to clean? Collecting is fun! I do it myself. I also dust weekly. Something to think about.
- Does it get in the way of your flow? Moving a framed photo off the top of your jewelry box each day in order to find pieces to accessorize

your outfit is not a great use of your time and energy. Especially if moving it starts a domino effect of having to move other things out of the way to set down the photo frame.
- Love everything you have. Remember that anything stored in a box is not worth having. If you have no room for it to be visible, consider making room by downsizing something else to make it fit.

Organizing is not sterile. I'm not asking you to live in a government-certified cleanroom. I'm not even asking you to live like a minimalist. **I'm suggesting that your quality of life is negatively impacted by disorder and greatly improved by order.** *Otherwise, truthfully, why are you reading this book?*

* * *

In a household of multiple people with multiple schedules requiring multiple things, things can and do get lost in the shuffle. Take for example my client Wanda who not only worked a full-time job but also was a single parent to two grade-school children and recently moved her elderly mother in with her. Stuff was going missing all the time! And it wasn't as if she was all that disorganized. The real problem was that she wasn't the one losing things...just the one who had to find them, usually at the worst possible moment.

Wanda and I started chatting one day at school pickup about our respective occupations and the pros and cons of each. She was a paralegal in DC and had the privilege of working from home three days a week. It's a deal she struck with the partners of the firm she had been with since college and one she was grateful to have. But she noted that working from home had its downfalls, especially when it came to separating the two.

"I could really use your help coming up with a plan. I have never felt like my house runs smoothly."

"Anytime. I'm happy to help."

"Are you free tomorrow morning?"

Wanda had a lovely three-level, two-bedroom townhouse in Wheaton, MD. It was a tight fit after moving her mother in, but she had managed to make space for everyone. The girls, aged five and seven, had already been sharing one of the two bedrooms and, for the moment, she was sharing her room with her mother. The plan was to convert the lower-level home office and storage room into a bedroom and living area with a small kitchenette for her mother. From there her mother would have access to the patio and fenced backyard for her bichon frise. The office was currently in boxes and Wanda was attempting to go through everything that had been in the storage room to determine what to keep and what to store in an offsite storage area along with her mother's things from her last home. The house was in flux and out of sorts but that wasn't what plagued Wanda. That part she could deal with because it was temporary. It was her girls and her mother who caused her the most stress. They were constantly misplacing things and creating shambles.

"My mother is a slob. Once she's moved in downstairs, her chaos should mostly stay with her. The kids are the real problem. They misplace things and then suddenly need those things as we're walking out the door. That's usually followed by a meltdown into tears and yelling. This whole situation has gotten away from me. I see you with your daughter always working as a team. Even the way she comes over to you at pickup. She doesn't throw her backpack at your feet and take off running for the playground. She places it in the backseat of the car and begins telling you about her day. I want that level of respect. It's really beautiful to watch."

I couldn't help but smile. My daughter and I ARE a good team and the fact that people saw that made me very proud of her and both of us.

"Thank you so much for saying that, Wanda. We work well together mostly because we have similar personalities. But I hear what you're saying and I'm happy to tell you how we do things in our world if you think it will help."

"I do and I know this is not your typical project but I don't expect you to dispense your advice for free. I want to pay whatever your time costs. Hourly is how I bill clients so I hope you'll agree to that."

"That works for me. Thank you. How about we meet at Starbucks next Tuesday after drop off?"

"Perfect. I'll meet you there."

Over the next week, I gave some real thought to my relationship with my daughter and how our household functioned. Was I just calling the shots and she fell in line? Was I up all night cleaning, organizing, and planning to keep my house running like clockwork? Was I stressing her out? Was I stressing myself out? *Yeah, I can go deep into a self-doubt spiral pretty fast.*

The truth was that I did call the shots, at first. And there were absolutely times that I was up all night cleaning, organizing, and planning. And I'm sure I had moments where I was stressing her out because I was definitely stressing myself out. But it all got easier. And then it became effortless—*though truthfully that post-college-year move home mess does put me in a bit of a tizzy that takes a few days to work through. I am who I am.*

I came up with a list of ideas for Wanda and her girls and even her mom. Things to try on and see if they fit. Things I hoped would create the order Wanda asked for but also the respect she craved. She was treading water and she was tired. And she felt taken for granted on top of it all. I wanted her to get to the point where some of the burden was taken off her shoulders, while still other burdens she just let go, **like that hateful idea of "perfection." There is no such thing, at least not universally and certainly never long held.**

I wanted her to strive for "better than good enough, approaching a personal ideal, wrapped up in happiness and contentment."

Organization requires a level of responsibility and respect that often goes unnoticed amongst the color-coordinated size-ordered life-in-pictures way that it is usually presented. We are responsible for how we respect the way we live. Regardless of background or education or financial wealth, living an organized life is universally achievable. But it's a choice.

If I buy the best couch I can afford and I spill food on it without cleaning properly or at all. If I don't correct the dog when it chews on the cushions. If I don't consistently remedy odors from smoking or bodies with neutralizing fabric spray. Then I am mistreating my possessions. In turn, I am wasting the money I spent on them, which also means I have disrespected the time it took me to earn that money. Now that is not to say you should cover your couch in plastic and rope off the room. What I'm saying is take care of your things. They may not last forever, things are rarely made to last that long, but they will last longer thereby extending their overall value. You may have heard the phrase, "It doesn't owe you a dime." It means that the amount of time a given item has served you exceeded the amount you paid for it. You got more than your money's worth and that is always a good thing.

Let's break this down in the style of that children's

favorite, *If You Give a Mouse a Cookie*. For those of you unfamiliar, you'll catch on.

> You work hard to earn money.
> The money you earn pays for the things in your home.
> If you treat those things well, they will last longer.
> If your things last longer, your money has gone further.
> If you treat those things poorly, they will need to be replaced sooner.
> If you need to replace them sooner, your money is not going as far as it could.
> Being organized is one way to extend the life of your belongings which makes your money go further and places more value on the time spent to earn that money.

"A-ha, but Bonnie, what about the time spent taking care of whatever thing you are talking about? How do you calculate that? Isn't that like putting more money toward that thing?"

Not really. That's where respect for your things and appreciation for the purpose they serve in your life comes into play. And that you can't put a price on. You take care of them and they will take care of you.

* * *

IDEAS FOR WANDA
Step One
- **Decide what YOU really want from this experience and make a list in "what I want" and "why" form.** Things like: I want the house to be neat so the chaos doesn't affect my mood and I won't be grouchy.

- **Make a list of what chores have to be done each day/week/month so that your household runs smoothly. Make another list of what you will be afforded the time to do once they are accomplished.** For example, daily: make beds, do dishes, check mail, do homework, straighten house, exercise; then I can go to bed with a clear mind knowing all will be well when I wake up.

This is a grand wishlist and I love lists! Check marks are momentum fuel. Make as many lists as you need to plan and plot on paper your perfectly precisioned world and then get to work. Refer to your lists often to keep everyone on the same page working together as a family, but feel free to make modifications as you go. Your lists are never set in stone.

Step Two
- With those lists in hand, **hold a family meeting**, preferably during or after a meal (*hunger*

and focus do not go together) with no outside distractions. You will discuss this new and exciting way you are all going to live where everyone feels proud and accomplished and will make everyone's lives easier and more efficient. No more looking for misplaced things at the last minute. No more procrastinating on schoolwork. The house will be more orderly and neat. And everyone will still have time for fun. More time, in fact.

- **Tell them that you are going to put together a plan for schoolwork and housework and benefits for each.** That as a family, you are going to make a list of projects you want to work on together and places to go as a family. That you are going to be firm but fair on respecting each other, your surroundings, and your stuff. That by working together to be more responsible, you'll become closer as a family.

- **Feel comfortable telling your kids that you are going to keep a closer eye on how money is being spent.** If everyone takes better care of their things, less money will go to replacing things that are lost or damaged. Learning how to budget and be responsible with money is a vital lesson to learn. Try to keep it light; doom and gloom about money troubles will create unnecessary fear. This is about learning respect for the time invested in earning as well as the skill to use money for true needs and wants and not whims *(at least not all the time)*.

- **Pull out a notebook and start taking suggestions for fun activities** both close to home and farther away, things that are free and things that cost money, and ways to make the things that cost money, cost less money *(like packing a picnic lunch instead of buying lunch when you go to the zoo for the day)*. Take down all suggestions for rewards from not having to do a particular nonessential chore one night during the week to a weekend at the beach.

- **Speak in an upbeat manner.** Smile. Tell them how proud you are of them for their positivity toward this new experience. Tell them how excited you are to get started, and then do it. Jump in with both feet to build on the positive energy.

- Then once the kids have gone to bed, **make your charts**. Whether you want a white board hung on a wall for everyone to see or you hold the master planner book, have fun with this too. This will become your nerve center for

EVERYTHING! The calendar, the chores, the goals, the rewards.

- Meet again once the charts are complete to discuss how they work, then **begin by doing something on the chart** to get started, right then and there.

- **Each morning in the car on the way to school set your agenda for the day in an upbeat way.** Discuss the day's events, expectations, and follow with a bit of daydreaming about the rewards. If everyone knows the plan upfront it doesn't feel so much like you are constantly telling them what to do. Send them off with a positive attitude for school. *I'm smiling now thinking that as my daughter got older she would be the one to send me off to work with an affirmation. Her favorite was "make good choices." It's surprising what your children pick up from you…be aware of that and make good choices.*

- Once you drop the kids at school, **begin your day with some deep centering breaths to focus on your own to-do list**. If you accomplish the bulk of your own tasks by the time you meet up with the kids later, you will be able to focus on encouraging them with their lists without being stressed about your own.

This is as much a reset for you as it is for them. You have to handle your business before you can show them how to handle theirs. *If airline instructions have taught us anything, it's that you put on your own mask before helping others put on theirs.*

Step Three
- As you continue with the process, **encourage them to try new things even if they don't get it exactly right**. Good enough is perfectly fine sometimes, as long as it gets done. Wouldn't it be wonderful to hear one summer morning, "Mommy, it's hot outside and your car is dirty. Can we wash it for you?" Accept that it may not be a great job, but then again, it may be fantastic. You won't know if you don't let them try. Perfection is not the goal. There are so many amazing things going on with this one offering to you and you allowing it without judgment. Enjoy it.

- **Encourage them to attempt to fix things for themselves with your guidance.** A moment of "Mommy, I'm not sure how to turn on the dishwasher. Can you watch me do it so I don't make a mistake?" is an opportunity to share a learning experience for both of you. They should be empowered to know that they can do hard things on their own but that you are there to help until they get better at it.

- **Explain that the "contract" they have with someone (their teachers, their friends, their family, even their belongings) must be respected in order to cultivate loving, working relationships.** *So the next time Kathleen forgets her homework, don't turn back to retrieve it. Let her go to school and explain what happened to her teacher. She will learn the consequences of her actions as well as being honest and advocating for herself.*

Make it fun! All of it! The work and the reward! Because if you're doing it together, it IS all fun!

Writing this section brought back so many happy memories of my daughter and I working as a team. Now that she's at college, we clearly don't have the time we used to, but when we do, we fall right back into it. In fact, the last time she was home for a few days, she said something so quintessentially "us" that it made my heart smile, "What's on the agenda for tomorrow?"

* * *

"Okay, I think I've got it. It can't make things any worse. My kids are monsters. I've lost control of my kids and my house and now my mom is with me and she adds to the heap plus she's always commenting on how bad the kids are. I just want to walk away and let them fend for themselves, you know?"

"That's not a terrible idea. Not the walking away part but the fending for themselves part. Let me ask you this, what was this morning like?"

"Madeline overslept and while I was trying to get her moving, Kathleen decided to make herself toast and burnt it. I asked my mom to help but she was struggling to get out of bed. Then we got halfway to school and AGAIN Kathleen said she left her homework at home so I had to turn around and get it. That's why I was late meeting you. We may be beyond control."

"Okay! You've had quite a morning. But no situation is really beyond help. Your girls are still little. You haven't ruined them yet," I laughed. "Let's back up for a second and talk about some ideas that may help you get a handle on things. If you are going to try to implement the ideas we just talked about, I would **speak to each family member individually to discuss their separate roles.**"

- I felt a conversation with her mother, as painful as it may be, would be the most straightforward and a great way to get her feet wet with this idea. Yes her mother was on the messy side, but soon enough she would have her own mini apartment downstairs complete with full bath, kitchenette, and access to the outside, so her things would mostly be contained. I suggested she not bring that up at all. What I did want her to discuss with her mother was her mother's support when it came to the kids, this new way of working together, and just having her back in general. Even if her mother didn't agree with her. Just one simple request to give this new lifestyle plan a fighting chance.

- Next, I thought that maybe she could take the girls one at a time out for an hour or so while the other stayed home with nana. This way, the focus would be between mother and child and not the dynamic of the sisters as a unit. I said I thought it best to speak to the child on their level and for their personality.

For example, Kathleen could be strong-willed, demanding, and bossy *(Wanda's words, not mine).* I suggested Wanda take that and cultivate Kathleen's leadership qualities. Say things like "leaders are kind, leaders care about the people they 'serve', that being a leader is not just about being in charge but encouraging others to be their best selves, and in order to do that she has to be responsible and lead by example."

> Then I asked Wanda what she thought about giving Kathleen more responsibility in the house, but not with regard to Madeline. Things like simple tasks and chores around the house as well as over herself.

- Lastly, Madeline. She was still little but she was learning by her sister's example and not her mother's. I suggested Wanda spend a bit more one-on-one time with 'Mads' so she didn't always feel like the third wheel to Wanda and Kathleen. In this way Wanda could regain some of the "mommy authority" that her eldest was imposing on the younger.

"Good ideas. I like it. What I'd like to do is work up the list over the next few days and then meet again to go over it. Does that work for you?"

"Absolutely. I'm free Friday morning. We could meet back here."

"Perfect. It's a date. And Bonnie, thank you. I really appreciate this."

"Of course. Anytime. I hope it all helps."

* * *

Wanda and I met that Friday and again on the following Tuesday to finalize her lists and what she would say to each of her family members. She was "cautiously optimistic." This was definitely a new organizing assignment for me and while I was looking forward to seeing how my advice would pan out, I certainly didn't want anyone to become lab rats to my parenting processes. I had my fingers crossed that this didn't come back to bite me.

The month that followed was crazy for me. My daughter was taking Ubers home more often than I was picking her up and so I wasn't running into Wanda at school. It had been nearly a month and a half since we last spoke. I was wary that things didn't go as well as I'd hoped when she didn't reach out to me and I didn't want to ask her about it. But one afternoon we did see each other in the parking lot of school. Before we could exchange pleasantries, her girls came out and gave her a hug. I heard Kathleen say, "C'mon mommy, we don't want to be late for the dentist" and took Wanda by the hand. She looked up at me and smiled, motioning that she would call me. I didn't need for her to call (though she did) because I could see it with my own eyes. It was happening for her. That peace and ease that comes from the well-oiled machinery of a family that works together as a team.

This was certainly organizing on a different level than most of my projects but order from chaos was found. And that is always my goal!

Extras

How to Streamline Housework

No one wants to clean but nearly everyone wants a clean house. How do you get it? Well, there is the option to hire cleaning services. Or you can do it yourself. Or you can let it get dirty. The last one is not really an option for a number of reasons, the least of which is you are reading a book about organizing so clearly you have some goals in mind that revolve around order.

If you have the option of hiring cleaning services, do. Even just once annually, if you can't justify the expense on a regular basis. Think of it as a yearly checkup, just to have someone do the heavy lifting *(both literally and figuratively)*. But during those times when you are handling the workload on your own, here are some ways to get it done, in less time, with less stress, and incorporate the sometimes unwilling participation of your family. It's all about perspective.

* * *

I've read and reread "The Miracle of Mindfulness" by the global spiritual leader Thich Nhat Hanh a few times now—*I will no doubt read it several more times because an organizer's brain is a forward-thinking-future-planning brain and struggles to live in the moment.* In it he writes many notable quotes but one hit me in such a way that I now apply it to my cleaning processes with anticipation *(yes, I see the contradiction).*

> *"While washing the dishes, you might be thinking about the tea afterwards, and so try to get them out of the way as quickly as possible in order to sit and drink tea. But that means that you are incapable of living during the time you are washing the dishes. When you are washing the dishes, washing the dishes must be the most important thing in your life. Just as when you're drinking tea, drinking tea must be the most important thing in your life...each act must be carried out in mindfulness."*

The point this Zen master is making is one of being present for the experience. Many of us think that living in the moment refers only to those joy-filled moments we don't want to miss, like slowing down to enjoy the sunset. What it actually means is to be focused on every part of every moment. **Don't waste any of it rushing through an action to get to another action you deem more worthy of your time and excitement. Enjoy**

How to Streamline Housework

it all. Give your attention and your enthusiasm to every task, including the chores.

1. **Small daily neatness habits make cleaning lighter.** Step one is easy to explain, perhaps more difficult to put into practice if it's not already part of your routine. Example: Instead of collecting discarded dirty laundry from the floor, the bed, the chair on laundry day, why not put it directly into the laundry basket when you take it off. The concept is so simple that it is completely ridiculous to write, but can anyone reading this say they haven't had to gather laundry on laundry day because it's not all in the hamper? I kind of doubt it.

2. **Do a little every day.** Rarely do we have the time to devote an entire day to cleaning. Nor do we want to. Break up the tasks. Mondays, bathroom and laundry. Tuesdays, upstairs vacuuming and dusting. Wednesday, kitchen appliances and countertops. You get the picture. Be sure to slot in housework projects that are monthly, quarterly, and annually too so you can plan ahead…mindfully of course.

3. **Prepare yourself to focus on the task at hand by eliminating all possible distractions.** Are the kids occupied and safe without

your undivided attention? Are you wearing work clothes you aren't worried about getting dirty or stained? *(I've got the bleach stains to prove my point.)* Is your hair up, your phone silenced, and your determination high, ready to tackle the job in front of you like a surgeon entering the OR?

4. **Gather all your supplies for the task at hand.** In Chapter 1 I explained at some length that I used to have all my cleaning supplies and instruments in one central location, but in doing that, I added an extra step to my chores. Remove that irritant by housing your cleaning supplies where you use them. A bucket of supplies in each bathroom, for example. *Or for me, I have a stepladder on each level of my three-level house so I can change lightbulbs, dust cobwebs, etc. and I don't have to lug a ladder up and down stairs.*

5. **Consider your tools and cleansers as part of an experiment.** Let me expand on the Master's example. You've been looking forward to reading a new book and you're going to make it a me-time event. You choose a tea, maybe even make a personal blend from loose leaves. You heat the water and begin steeping. Maybe you get a little fancy and pull out the

good china. Slice a fresh, plump lemon. Find the organic honey you bought on that trip to Vermont years ago. Forage for your stash of special cookies in the back of the pantry and place two, okay maybe three, on a plate. Tea is finished steeping so you complete the tea preparation and you take a breath to appreciate this beautiful tray of treats. You carry it to your favorite comfy chair. Get yourself tucked in, light at the right angle, warm blanket, book in lap, you take that first sip of tea letting the steam and aroma waft over your face as you close your eyes and drink in the full experience.

BUT, before the tea came the chore. The chore you rushed through to get to the tea. Try to apply the same attention to detail and enjoyment to the procedures there. Rinse the plates, arrange them in the dishwasher, choose your detergents, decide on a washing cycle, close the door, hit start, wipe down the dishwasher of errant crumbs or water drops, wipe down the counter, wash the sink, run the garbage disposal, rehang your dish towel, shut off the light. Done. Mindfulness is in the procedure, in the dance, in the meditation of the task. And in doing so, you live each moment, in the moment, instead of treating it as a burden to endure to get to the tea.

* * *

So how exactly does this streamline housework? The work is still there and it's not going anywhere. That's a fact. BUT by changing how you approach housework, you streamline housework:

- by changing your habits so there is less work to your work
- by breaking work down into manageable tasks
- by preparing thoughtfully for the task at hand
- by planning ahead for ease of procedures
- and by focusing on your motions in a mindful, joyful way

The work then doesn't feel like a drudgery or a task to get through and get over with. It in itself brings you happiness and in that way it's all part of a positive, effortless, streamlined lifestyle.

It Bears Repeating: Excerpt from Chapter 1 of "Stop Buying Bins"

If you have more clothes than space, these are **the questions to ask yourself as you downsize.** Be honest

Excerpt from Chapter 1 of "Stop Buying Bins"

here. If you are not wearing or cannot wear something you own, it has to go!

- **Does it fit?** If the answer is "no", there is nothing more to think about. Put it in a big green garbage bag earmarked for the donation center and don't look back.

If it does fit:
- **Is it in any way damaged—stained, faded, missing fasteners, misshapen by wash, etc.?**
- **Does it look good on you?**
- **Do you wear it regularly?**
- **Have you worn it recently?**
- **Is it still tagged after months in your closet?**
- **Do you honestly have any use for it?**
- **Would someone you know get better use out of it?**
- **Did you need it at some point but no longer need it?**
- **Did you buy it on sale because it was on sale?**
- **Did you forget you had it?**
- **Do you still like it?**
- **Have you read through all of these questions and still are saying "but it's still good"?**
    Well then, you know what I'm going to say now.

Last point I'd like to reiterate. You've pulled it all

out. You've asked yourself the right questions. You've made your piles and sent off a good percentage of clothes onto their next adventure. Now you're starting each day with this renewed wardrobe. But you still somehow keep bypassing that yellow button-down shirt. It fits, you have reason to wear it, and it's in good condition. But it's not in the rotation. **Either work it onto the team roster or make it a free agent.** We're not keeping things for no good reason anymore. Use it or lose it.

Bottom line, these are clothes. Most of us don't have bespoke designer Met Gala–worthy duds made of archival silk spun by magic fairies. Our clothes came from a store off a rack with thousands of other identical pieces. Letting go of them is not all that difficult precisely for that reason—they are replaceable. What cannot be replaced, however, is physical space in your home, time spent getting dressed, self-respect when you feel unattractive or defeated, and money lost on useless purchases. Don't punish yourself for growing old, gaining weight, making impulse buys, or holding onto things past their point of usefulness. Instead, let go of the triggering item, absolve yourself of the error in judgment, and give yourself permission to be who you are now in this moment. Nothing is more important when it comes to your clothes, or your life for that matter, than feeling comfortable and confident with yourself.

My Take on Swedish Death Cleaning

I have been witness to more personal struggles, of clients attempting to free themselves from the mass of possessions left in their care after a loved one passes, than I care to count. It is physically, emotionally, and psychologically exhausting for everyone involved. And as someone from the outside looking in, it's frustrating. For every client grieving the loss of a family member, they are simultaneously simmering with disappointment, sometimes even anger, that they have been left to deal with the aftermath.

I am going to take this opportunity to be blunt whether you want to hear it or not. The truth is you are not going to live forever and admitting it to yourself or saying it out loud will not "tempt fate." You will pass away at some point, I hope after a long and happy life, but then all that will truly be left is how you are remembered. Don't stain your memory by having those you leave behind have to deal with your possessions. Because here's the painful truth: most of it is going to wind up in the trash. I've lost count of how many times I have witnessed this event. A dumpster or two will be wheeled in and for days, even weeks, the things in your home you just couldn't part with or willingly chose not to deal with, will be let go in the most brutal fashion, right into the garbage. And those of whom you left doing the work, well, let's just say, the memory of you doesn't shine quite as bright as it once did. That is, unless you do something about it NOW, here, in this moment, when you can be in control of your destiny and, far more importantly, in control of your legacy.

Swedish Death Cleaning:
a method of organizing and decluttering your home before you die to lessen the burden on your loved ones after you've passed.

In many ways, this is not about the deceased at all. It is about the gift you leave. Gift. That's an interesting way to look at this scenario. What you leave behind is the last gift, the ultimate gift to your family. You may argue that your memory is the gift, family ties, commitment to the bonds of friendship, and the like. When your loved ones are presented with your final present, will it be wrapped in clutter they must wade through to receive it or given without effort or burden attached so they can grieve properly.

* * *

I've had the responsibility of downsizing many clients as they move to smaller homes. I have gently attempted to broach the subject of downsizing as an end-of-life scenario so as not to place the awesome task on their heirs. I've heard varied responses all saying the same thing:

- They can do what they want with it.
- They can just throw out what they don't want.
- They can deal with it when I'm gone.
- I don't want to talk about dying.
- Sadly, this lays all the weight on those who are grieving.
- Consider taking a different perspective:
- Let's have them take what they want now.
- Let's go through what is really disposable and donate, sell, or gift now.
- Let's not put the family through more after I'm gone.
- I want to know my family is taken care of when, one day down the road, I won't be able to take care of them.

* * *

So let's assume you have chosen to embrace this moment as an opportunity to relieve the toll your possessions will take on your family one day. Swedish Death Cleaning is not unlike typically downsizing with one exception—it considers those most important to you and what you would like to give them in memory of you. What follows is how I would approach the task at hand with my client in a methodical and efficient manner, always bearing in mind the emotional toll this project takes.

For purposes of storyline, my "client" is an 83-year-old woman, widowed in the last five years, with two grown children and multiple grandchildren all living within an hour radius. She is moving from the large family home she has lived in for 50+ years to a retirement community of her own choice and she is overwhelmed with how to proceed in downsizing her possessions. There is a great deal of clutter in the home ranging from antique furniture to basic recyclables. But she is willing and ready to participate in this process and has asked for my guidance.

1. **Determine what will be moved to the new home. One of my favorite activities in any downsizing project is to "shop from your stock!"** In this instance, however, we are really going to raise the bar on fun! Instead of searching for that one underused item that you can put to use in a new way, you get to shop for an entire household of things with fresh eyes. To level up the excitement of this perspective switch, make it a shopping spree.

    a. Write out a shopping list for your new home with all the items and quantities you will need of each. For example: dishes (6 place settings only or 12 dinner plates only), lamps (3 table lamps and 1 floor lamp), blankets (2 throw blankets, 1 comforter, 1 quilt), always bearing in mind the needs of your new lifestyle and size of your new space.

b. Take a look at all your belongings. Walk from room to room with a single focus. For example: only paying attention to table lamps. Just like you are shopping in a store.

c. Once you've seen your selection throughout your house, refer to your shopping list. For example: you need 3 table lamps and 1 floor lamp. Place a sticker on those lamps throughout the house that will be moving with you.

d. Bear in mind that you are downsizing, so if you currently have four beds in your four-bedroom house, you will only need one. You cannot take all four. But what you can do is choose the one you want to take and it doesn't have to be the one you were using.

2. Ideally, if you have the option, move the items you are taking to your next home, to your next home. If they can't be moved out, move them to a common location within the house so they are no longer scattered in different rooms.

3. **The remaining items are "in play." That does not mean they are all destined for the landfill; in fact, please try not to do that. Instead, consider the following:**

   a. Have your children remove anything that is personally theirs. Clothes, books, school memorabilia. *In all honesty, it should have been moved out with them years before but no time like the present. P.S. They should take it ALL even if they don't want it. They can dispose of it from their own homes.*

   b. Have your family and friends over for dinner and "shopping." I've done this several times throughout my adult life and I can attest that there is something so gratifying in seeing someone you love find something they want that you can gift to them effortlessly.

   c. Do not force anyone to take what they do not want because you think they should have it. Likewise for your family and friends, do not keep anything you do not want that is given to you because someone else felt you should have it.

   d. An even distribution of goods between your loved ones is not a factor here. This experience is not the same as dividing your estate equally amongst your children. This experience is about three things: downsizing the possessions you cannot take to your next home, witnessing someone receiving joy from an item you no longer have use for, and weeding out those items no one cares about, now, before the grieving process takes place. Equality comes down to all your loved ones having an equal opportunity to take what they'd like. That's the even distribution.

e. Everything that remains should be filtered yet again into saleable, donation, and trash. Yes, there will be trash. Not everything in your home is worth the effort it takes to sell or even donate. *Christmas lights that don't light come to mind.*

4. **Take out the trash. Recycle what you can. Do it right away before it becomes part of the decor.**

5. **Host an estate sale or sell online.**

6. **Schedule a donation pickup or make multiple trips to the donation center.**

7. **Are there still some items left? Have your family, friends, even neighbors back for more dinner and shopping.**

8. **The last of it will have to be donated or trashed. Of course, anything on the front lawn with a "FREE" sign works too.**

Always keep the following in mind whether you are downsizing or death cleaning *(they really do need to come up with a better name; it's the name that's off-putting, not the experience)*. Look at your things and say to yourself:

- I have everything I need. This is all extra. I am finished with telling myself I need things I do not.
- I have all that I want. This isn't what I want. I want for little, this is too much.
- These are just things taking up space. My space. I will not continue to allow them a place of honor in my home.
- If I say to myself "I have to have it," then I must use it, love it, see it, cherish it.
- I'm not holding onto things just because they cost me money. I clearly wasted that money. I don't need to be reminded of that.
- Giving feels good. Even better than buying. Monumentally better than just having.
- This experience right now gives me the rare opportunity to spend time with my family, enjoying memories and sharing in our abundance.

- I'm thinking about my family, left with the task of dealing with this lifetime of my possessions. If they want it, I want to witness them enjoying it, now while I still can.
- It is not morbid to think about my death. It is responsible and caring. I will not leave this burden behind.

Do this for your family. Do this for your loved ones. Do this for yourself when you can be present with your presence and your presents.

Keep Your Disorganized Life to Yourself

[WARNING! MAY OFFEND SOME; OTHERS WILL TOTALLY GET IT; STILL OTHERS MAY SEE IT FOR THE WAKE-UP CALL IT IS!]

Get ready! I'm not pulling any punches with this little chapter. You've read this book almost all the way to the end so you know by now how much I like to use examples. Well here's a doozy for you. It's slightly off-topic from "home" organizing but it does hit at one of the root traits behind the personality of someone who is disorganized. Read on. And if it strikes a cord, breathe and consider why.

Stop Pushing Perfection

PERSON A

Person A's alarm clock went off at 6am but they were already waking up. They brushed their teeth and their hair, made their bed, and made "the rounds" of the house, turning off outdoor lights and unplugging fully charged items from overnight. With the Keurig turned on and their laptop opened, they replied to emails, sent texts, and read news highlights while brewing a cup of coffee. Taking both back to their desk, they checked their daily calendar and rearranged the day to suit the weather. (*Raining out: no need to water the flowers; plan morning meetings accordingly to account for possible rain-related traffic.*) A scroll through social media and a quick look at business stats, followed by some breakfast, washing the dishes, getting dressed, doing one or more household cleaning tasks for that specific day *(quick organize the refrigerator and pantry; make a shopping list)*, then settling in to write with a second cup of coffee. They have a 9:15am meeting 20 minutes away which means they must leave by 8:55am. Building in an extra 5 minutes for hiccups plus 20 minutes to put on some makeup and style hair, they can write until 8:30am. Plenty of time for edits since it's only 7:45am. Not wanting to make the meeting partner wait, Person A builds in another 5-minute buffer and arrives at 9:07am for the meeting, carrying the materials needed that they picked up the day before so there was no need to rush in the morning. I think we all know who Person A is. But they didn't get that way by accident. Some of it is personality, some of it is habit, some of it is respect for others.

PERSON B

Person B woke up at 8:30am having forgotten to set the alarm clock the night before. They went downstairs and made a cup of coffee and breakfast. Sat down and flipped through a magazine on the table. It's now 9:05am. They need to be at a 9:15am meeting 20 minutes away *(clearly they will be late)* so they get dressed, including makeup and hair. They head for the door but can't find their car keys. It is now 9:45am. Phone rings and it's their meeting partner wondering if the reason they are late is that they are picking up the materials for the meeting. Person B says they are leaving the house now, will pick up the materials on the way, and be there in 30 minutes *(an impossibility with rain, traffic, and still having to pick up materials, not to mention they haven't yet found their car keys).* At 10am, the meeting partner cancels the meeting. Person B eventually finds the keys, picks up the materials, and brings them to the canceled meeting but no one is there *(because, well, the meeting was canceled).* They leave a note implying it was rude that the meeting was canceled because they have now arrived with the materials. It is 11:15am. Person B is disorganized and their disorganization affects others. But they didn't get that way by accident. Some of it is personality, some of it is habit, some of it is disrespect for others.

Don't be like Person B.

From those of us who are organized to those of you who are not, do better! Your actions speak volumes and it is all saying one thing: "I'm more important than you!" If you don't think it's important to be organized for yourself, then at least do it for those around you. Sure, you like to be all "loosy-goosy and fly by the seat of your pants because it's cool not to care," but you're being a selfish jerk! Harsh? Well, if you want to be disorganized on your own time, have at it. But the moment you commit to a plan with others, you have to follow through. Anything else is self-involved, passive-aggressive, and just plain rude. I'll say it again—don't be like Person B.

An Organized Life Simplifies

Whether you live in a one-room cabin in some remote woodland or a 10-bedroom penthouse in a major city; whether you are mega-wealthy or barely scraping by; whether you live alone or in a multigenerational home of many; none of that prevents you from living an efficient and organized life.

And you want to know why?

Because being organized saves you time and money. Being organized means:

An Organized Life Simplifies

- You always have a plan.
- You have what you need to implement your plan.
- You are prepared to shift gears when issues arise.
- You rarely misplace things.
- And since you don't misplace things, you don't waste time looking for them or money replacing them.
- You rarely run out of things.
- And since you don't run out of things, you don't waste time and energy getting last-minute replacements.
- You are rarely late.
- And if you are running late, you alert all parties involved so they are informed.
- But since you're rarely running late, you never have to rush.
- When work needs to be done, you do it methodically and efficiently.
- By working methodically, there is less opportunity for error.
- By working efficiently, the work is done in less time.
- And since work takes less time, there is more time for activities you love.
- Your home is always efficient, if not also neat and clean.

- And since it's always efficient, getting it both neat and clean are easier tasks.
- You keep a calendar of regularly scheduled appointments for yourself, your family, and your property to keep them all in proper health and working order.
- Since you and your family receive regular checkups, you are prepared ahead of time for any changes to your health and therefore can prepare for any issues.
- And since your home and property are well maintained, both require fewer major repairs or replacements, saving both time and money.
- Plus, you appreciate your home and property more because they are well maintained. Gratitude is a bonus byproduct of being organized.
- All of which gives you more time to enjoy the company of your family and friends...

and all by living an organized life.

Not one of the above bullet points is influenced by bank account, family size, or square footage of your home. Anyone can live an organized lifestyle, and in doing so, will without any doubt in my mind, live an easier (read happier) life.

I can't say I know what it feels like to be disorganized. It's just not in my nature. But does my own

An Organized Life Simplifies

house get out of sorts? Of course! So don't beat yourself up if you fall into old habits, but don't let it prevent you from getting yourself together in the first place. Here's the upside. Once you've organized and put systems in motion, even if things get out of hand, the basis for order is still underneath everything. You are not starting from scratch. You just have to put it back together. The more you work within the system, the better your habits will get, and the longer you will go before the next slip. And we ALL slip. Myself included. I'll give you an example. You would be surprised to see the cobwebs that are in my house right now. I'm short so I rarely notice those whispery strands floating above my head. But seeing as this is the last sentence of the book, I suppose there's no time like the present to grab the long-handled duster and get to work.

A Note To Booksellers:

STOP PUSHING PERFECTION is the second in a series about efficient living and is specifically focused on organizing, lifestyle systems, and practical decor. My first book, *STOP BUYING BINS,* focused on downsizing to get the reader to the point where they could apply the subjects covered in this book. In my role as a professional home organizer and interior decorator, I repeatedly found that setting up the picture of organized perfection bears little resemblance to setting up a workable, streamlined living space, learning the systems to manage it efficiently, and applying practical decor principles so your space is both beautiful and functional.

I would be so grateful if you would carry this book in your store. And I hope you enjoy reading it as much as I enjoyed writing it. Thank you for your consideration.

www.ingramcontent.com/pod-product-compliance
Lightning Source LLC
Chambersburg PA
CBHW070502120526
44590CB00013B/731